Why Should Anyone Believe Anything at All?

JAMES W. SIRE

INTERVARSITY PRESS
DOWNERS GROVE, ILLINOIS 60515

InterVarsity Press® is the book-publishing division of InterVarsity Christian Fellowship®, a student movement active on campus at hundreds of universities, colleges and schools of nursing in the United States of America, and a member movement of the International Fellowship of Evangelical Students. For information about local and regional activities, write Public Relations Dept., InterVarsity Christian Fellowship, 6400 Schroeder Rd., P.O. Box 7895, Madison, WI 53707-7895.

All Scripture quotations, unless otherwise indicated, are taken from the HOLY BIBLE, NEW INTERNATIONAL VERSION®. NIV®. Copyright © 1973, 1978, 1984 by International Bible Society. Used by permission of Zondervan Publishing House. All rights reserved.

Excerpt from The Historical Reliability of the Gospels by Craig Blomberg. ©1987 Craig L. Blomberg. Used by permission of InterVarsity Press, Downers Grove, IL, U.S.A., and Inter-Varsity Press, Leicester, England.

Cover illustration: Kurt Mitchell

ISBN 0-8308-1397-7
Printed in the United States of America ♾

Library of Congress Cataloging-in-Publication Data

Sire, James W.
    Why should anyone believe anything at all?/James W. Sire.
        p.   cm.
    Includes bibliographical references.
    ISBN 0-8308-1397-7
    1. Belief and doubt.   2. Apologetics—20th century.   3. Jesus
Christ—Person and offices.   I. Title.
BD215.S55   1994
239—dc20   94-18632
                                                            CIP

---

17   16   15   14   13   12   11   10   9   8   7
08   07   06   05   04   03   02   01   00

To
the students who have
listened to me, probed, inquired
and sometimes confused me,
but always stimulated me to do
better next time

Preface

This book has been a long time in the making. In 1982 David Suryk, staff member with InterVarsity Christian Fellowship serving the campus of Illinois State University, invited me to give a lecture on why one should believe the Christian faith. That lecture, given under the title "Is Christianity Rational?" sparked enough discussion in response that I repeated it at the University of Rochester the following academic year. At the end of that lecture a student stood and asked if he could read something. When I asked him how long it was, he said two pages. The comments he had prepared in anticipation to show that Christianity could not be considered rational kept a formal discussion going for several hours. Obviously this topic was hitting a nerve.

A few months later still, students at Harvard University asked me to give the lecture again. This time they advertised it by appending a number of questions in addition to the title question. One of these was "Why should anyone believe anything at all?" I saw immediately that this was the key question. I had been dealing with the issue in the way suggested by this question anyway. All I had to do was change the title.

In the past ten years I have presented the material over 150 times in universities in the United States and Canada, and even once each in Bulgaria, Slovakia, Croatia, Hungary and the Czech Republic.

In 1989, InterVarsity staff members Mark and Gwen Potter conducted a survey of students at Swarthmore, Haverford and Bryn Mawr using the single question "Why should anyone believe anything at all?" The results were so interesting that this survey has been repeated at some thirty other universities. Most of the quotations from students in the pages that follow come from these surveys. These surveys were not conducted in such a way that statistical conclusions should be drawn. Still, the responses provide a rare insight into what some students are thinking about the reasons they and others believe.

"Why should anyone believe anything at all?" gets beneath the truth of any one religion. It raises the issue of why we believe *anything*, from simple daily matters to the perennial eternal issues that ground our very lives. It makes us realize that it is not just Christians and religious people who believe. Atheists and agnostics do so too. Moreover, belief is fundamental to all human action, not just religion. We even believe in order to eat. But more of this in chapters to come.

The book is divided into two parts: (1) why one should believe anything and (2) why anyone should believe Christianity. In the lecture/discussion from which this book is generated, I am able only to skim the surface of the second issue; so I have developed part two by using and expanding on materials I have used in other lectures.

No argument for any fundamental belief will be convincing for everyone. So I have not tried to construct such an argument. I have instead tried to present the argument that at this point in my life is most convincing first to me and then to university students and graduates. For me (and I would wish this were so for all university students and graduates) it is important that an argument for belief (1) be based on the best evidence, (2) be validly argued and (3) refute the strongest objections that can be made. Some arguments have tremendous emotional force without much in the way of rational relevance. I have tried to avoid these.

As will become clear in what follows, I do not believe that any of us can have absolute philosophic certitude. Nonetheless, I do believe that we can have access to the truth. Lesslie Newbigin has put it better than anyone I know. "Visions of reality," he says, commend themselves to us by their "beauty, rationality, and comprehensiveness."

The acceptance of such a vision is a personal act, an act of personal judgment to which one commits oneself in the knowledge that others may disagree and that one may be proved wrong. It involves personal commitment. But it is not therefore merely subjective. The scientist who commits himself to the new vision does so—as Polanyi puts it—with universal intent. He believes it to be objectively true, and he therefore causes it to be widely published, invites discussion, and seeks to persuade his fellow scientists that it is a true account of reality. . . . At no stage is it merely a subjective opinion. It is held "with universal intent" as being a true account of reality which all people ought to accept and which will prove itself true both by experimental verification and also by opening the way to fresh discovery. It is offered not as private opinion but as public truth.[1]

Like Newbigin, I believe that we can come to grasp some of the truth. We may make mistakes. We may have to change our mind. But our beliefs must not be relegated to the status of private opinion. The only thing worth believing is the truth. When we believe we have apprehended the truth, we can hold it with universal intent.

Finally, I do not want to leave the impression that we are solely on our own in determining the truth. God is always present as Creator of the universe, of others and of ourselves. As the Logos, he has endowed us with a mind that is capable of grasping something of the truth about himself, his universe and ourselves.[2] We are both finite and fallen, and our mental equipment is flawed. Still, the Holy Spirit is present in whatever way he wishes, and he woos us toward the truth, illuminates our mind and confirms our feeble grasping after the truth. He does this, I believe, not in spite of our attempts at careful thought but through these attempts. The Holy Spirit is not a part of our arguments; he is not a "reason" for our belief. He is rather the final context in which our minds and hearts rest. He is why we can make progress toward believing that which is true.

Behind the whole argument of this book, then, is the assumption that God is present with us and to us both when we know it and when we don't. As the Word (Logos, John 1:1-4), he is the creative source of our ability to understand and believe the truth. As the Spirit of truth (John 1:9), he enables us to see the truth of good arguments.

I did not become a believer through an argument like the one set forth in this book. I was too young even to understand it. I became a believer because what was presented to me appeared true. On the basic issues at stake then—who I was, who God was, what he had done for me, what I was to do about that—I have made no basic changes. I believe much more in quantity and, I trust, in detail and quality. But I do not believe differently.

I have tried throughout to be cautious and fair both to the complexity of the issues addressed and to those whose work I have consulted, criticized, accepted and generally learned much from. So many so wise have treated these issues so well. I owe them much. I also owe much to the students who have attended the lectures in which this material was presented and who took time to respond to surveys.

Finally, I want to acknowledge the insights of several readers: David Suryk, Dan Reid and Douglas Groothuis. At a critical stage, conversations with Tim Peebles and David Wright were helpful. Thanks too go to my editor, Jim Hoover, who has over the years prevented my publishing especially poor books when I could do better. And a final thanks to Ruth Goring Stewart, who put the final polish on the text. Whatever errors remain are, alas, my own.

May what follows here help readers clarify for themselves the most important issues any of us face!

Why Should Anyone Believe Anything?

Part I

Basically it seems impossible to not believe in anything.
Such an adventure would lead one spiraling into the complete
uncertainty that Descartes experienced in his meditations.
Even if one believes that one should not believe, that is, of course,
something. It is the way the human mind works. Everyone needs a
central reference point, and some sort of belief serves that.

BRYN MAWR STUDENT, 1989

* * *

There is no "why" about it. We cannot help but believe things.
It is the way we were constructed. You might as well ask,
Why should unsupported objects fall? Or, Why should
addition be commutative? We can choose what to believe,
but not whether to believe.

OBERLIN STUDENT, 1991

It Makes My Head Hurt: The Nature & Necessity of Belief

1

O h, no! There's that question again! I've seen it all over campus.
It makes my head hurt." This was the agonized response of a
student at the University of Tennessee.

Posters had been widely displayed around the campus, asking a
question and announcing a lecture: "Why Should Anyone Believe
Anything at All?" At the same time a group of students conducted a
survey, asking the same question. This student had just come upon the
survey team standing at a desk in the student union.

He put his hands to his head and walked away. A few minutes later
he returned. Those conducting the survey handed him a sheet of
paper and asked him for his response. He took it, pondered for a few
moments, then thrust it back. "I can't do it. I can't do it," he said and
walked away.

Belief on Automatic Pilot
What makes the question "Why should anyone believe anything at

all?" so problematic? I think it's because it strikes at the very heart of who we are as human beings. It raises for us a question we just don't ordinarily ask ourselves.

We believe. That's what we do to live. Believing is like breathing: we do it, but we only know we are doing it when something draws our attention to it. Most of the day we simply breathe automatically. Then we play tennis and get short of breath, our breathing becomes problematic, and we notice it.

So too with believing. Suddenly someone asks us why we are doing it and we are at a loss. *I do believe,* we say to ourselves. I believe lots of things. From the simple matter of believing that my computer will work when I turn it on to the much more questionable belief that my broker is honest or my fiancée loves me in ways she loves no one else, everything I do is predicated on belief. Sometimes I question my beliefs—especially the complex ones, the ones involving people, life goals, politics and religion. But I always have them. Belief is automatic.

It is when someone asks me, "Why *should* I believe *anything* at all?" that the trouble comes home. Many students, when asked this question, simply retort, "Why not?" or "Because!" These responses I take to be casual attempts either to be humorous or to be rid of the questioner—understandable enough in a world of hucksters peddling wares by taking surveys.

Still, if we take the question seriously, it can drive us backwards into a slough of despond. We certainly take many things about life on face value; usually we are not disappointed. But ask us to prove even to ourselves that we are right in our belief, and we are in a quandary. Some go as far as Chuang Chou, the ancient Chinese philosopher:

> How can I tell you why I am so or why I am not so? Once I, Chuang Chou, dreamed that I was a butterfly and was happy as a butterfly. I was conscious that I was quite pleased with myself, but I did not know that I was Chou. Suddenly I awoke, and there I was, visibly Chou. I do not know if it was Chou dreaming that he was a butterfly or the butterfly dreaming that it was Chou.[1]

Was this what the student from the University of Tennessee had been pondering? Was he struck by the human condition? Did he see that we must believe because if we can't know who we ourselves are, we can't know *anything* with intellectual certitude? Was he caught in a house of mirrors—plagued, like Chuang Chou, by an infinite regress of whys? Perhaps. And perhaps he was in a better position than those with a naive belief in themselves and their own ability to make sense of the world.

One student from the University of North Carolina—Chapel Hill wrote:

If you don't believe in anything at all, I'd guess you lead a pretty bleak existence. I think it's really important to believe in yourself. Once you know who you are and where you're going, things seem to fall into place. Personally, I don't believe in God. I believe in people and I believe in nature and that's enough for me. I believe enough in myself to know that I will be as moral as I need to be— for me—without having to follow some other law (say, the Ten Commandments). I also believe that other people will behave in a moral way for them because I don't believe that people are inherently evil. I think everybody's pretty decent, as matter of fact. And this world—with all its "isms" and faults—is still a pretty [expletive deleted] cool place to be!

One can certainly agree with the first sentence: life without belief would be bleak. But to dismiss belief in God and opt for belief in oneself is either to trivialize the search for meaning or to indulge in the highest form of arrogance. The tone of the remarks suggests the former. Here is the happy hedonist whose religion is himself/herself. Perhaps such a stance can be maintained for a few months on a university campus by a first-year student. But it is bound eventually to come up against a very different reality. Then what?

We can with much reason ask the question: Why *should* anyone believe what this student believes? What justification is there for thinking that everyone is as moral as they need to be for themselves? Or for thinking that others are as moral as they need to be for others?

Is everybody really "pretty decent"? One wants to ask the student, What universe have you been living in? Are you not Chuang Chou's butterfly dreaming you are a college student in North Carolina?

The Subtlety of Belief
The fact is that belief is a subtle matter—much more subtle than most of us suppose.[2] But subtle as it is, we cannot leave its analysis to the experts. We need to understand for ourselves, at whatever level of intellectual ability, why it is we do believe, why we must believe and why we should believe one thing rather than another. For everyone with intellectual integrity and curiosity, this subject is too important to be left to the pros.

This chapter begins, then, to examine some of the basic parameters of the topic. Though the discussion will touch on a variety of areas—practical living, science and technology—I will be especially attentive to the issues that relate to religious belief.

Take an illustration from practical living. We believe the milk is fresh when we pour it in the glass; we recognize our mistake when we begin to drink it. We have started with a belief based on past experience, of course. We have acted on that belief, and we have found ourselves mistaken. Quite an ordinary occurrence, to be sure.

But do we recognize that what looked like an application of simple basic reason is itself based on belief, actually at least two beliefs? First, we trust our senses: we believe what our taste tells us. Second, we trust our reason to draw the proper conclusion from the sense of taste. In a strict sense, we can actually prove neither one. Every test for the validity of our senses relies on our senses themselves. Every test for reason relies on reason.

We can test the performance of our senses against a standard outside our own senses. For example, we can ask a friend to taste the milk. But there is no standard outside human taste for human taste. Likewise we can ask a friend whether she thinks the milk is sour. Actually she might say, "No, it's fresh milk, but it's from a dairy that gets its supply from a special kind of cow. Its milk just tastes different.

You'll get used to it and learn to like it!"

Even scientists rely on assumptions that cannot finally be proved.[3] First, there is the assumption that the physical universe is uniform: if water boils at 100 degrees Celsius today, then under the same circumstances it would have done so yesterday and forever in the past and will do so tomorrow and forever in the future. Second is the assumption that the uniformity is rational, capable of being grasped by the human mind. Third is the assumption that our senses—the ones we use to "read" the data from the instruments we use—are generally reliable. We see what is really there. Fourth, we assume that our reason is capable of reaching valid conclusions, based on accurate data. In the formation of new theories, scientists also trust their creative imagination to stretch beyond the data to formulate new hypotheses that can later be checked for consistency and coherence with what is already held to be true or that give a better explanation of the data than previously established theories.

The practical effect of using these assumptions has been the development of ever more comprehensive theories and the production of explanations that have practical consequences. In other words, making these assumptions has allowed human beings to gain more and more control over the environment. In short, science works. This tends at least to confirm the practical value of science. That is, scientists are clearly justified in assuming the truth of their assumptions. In fact, scientists are *psychologically certain* that these assumptions are true. They simply never—or very, very rarely—doubt them. In the final analysis, though, science's success does not prove with final *philosophical certitude* that the assumptions are true.

A student from Hunter College put it well:

All rational thought is based on premises, and these premises must be if not actually *believed*, then at least accepted. Even a conviction about the power of reason itself is an act of faith. Hence it is impossible to believe in nothing at all.

Then, what about belief in the religious realm? How do we know if there is a God, or what happens after death, or whether we are obligated to any sort of deity? Is there a purpose or meaning to human existence? Why are we here? Why am I here? *What should* we believe about these sorts of questions? And *why should* we believe anything at all about them—why believe they are important even to consider?

Whatever else one can say, these are the sorts of questions people have been asking and trying to answer as far back as we can trace. Their permanence as questions confirms their importance. It isn't just those who read the scandal sheets who have "inquiring minds." Aristotle said it most clearly: "All men by nature desire to know."[4] And we will not stop with questions about the world around us. We will also seek our origins, our ends and our meaning.[5]

Over the millennia people have answered these questions in a wide variety of ways. Some parallel each other, some touch at a few points, others are in diametrical opposition. Long before the twentieth century, it became obvious that these questions were so vast, so encompassing, that answering them with confident certitude demands a sort of omniscience no mere human being has or could ever possess. Only a few people on the very margins of society—people in mental institutions, for example—claim to have this sort of knowledge on their own. Most people, including most people of any religious persuasion, hold that the answers to these questions are in the final analysis a matter of belief.

To be sure, just how belief relates to reason, how much we are able to know with a high measure of philosophic certitude, how much we have to accept on faith—whether blind or partially or heavily informed—has been a matter for debate over the centuries. Still, there is a large measure of agreement that some things are more worthy of belief than others.

The Far Edge of Death

Before we get too abstract, we should look at an example of the sorts of issues about which belief is required. Let's look at the question, What happens to a person at death?

Many people believe that after death every human being will be reincarnated. Many others reject this notion and instead believe that each person will be resurrected to a bodily existence in a higher realm of reality. Others believe that at death the soul takes up existence in a spiritual plane parallel to the physical plane. Still others believe that all that is uniquely personal ceases to exist at physical death; there is no soul to be reincarnated or resurrected or transformed to a spirit.

It is important to note that these various views cannot all be true.[6] They are mutually contradictory.[7] Either there is something uniquely human that survives death or there is not. It can't go both ways. And if there is something that survives, then reincarnation and resurrection rule out each other. Resurrection requires the continuation of the unique personhood of the one who died: Jane stays Jane after death and resurrection. Reincarnation requires that this not be the case; each soul becomes a different individual: Jane can become Jack or Jill, Juan or Juanita, in a further incarnation. It makes no sense for one of us to say, "Resurrection is true for you; reincarnation is true for me." If one is true, the other is not.[8]

The problem we face is this: none of the various views of what happens at death can be proved with final philosophical certitude. One can always imagine that some part of the data is inadequate or in error, or that something of the reasoning is invalid. Even though I have no reason not to believe something, I can still—in my heart of hearts—doubt what is offered. Regardless of the view, I must take it with some amount of faith. Whatever I hold, I must *believe*. So the questions return: given all the options regarding death, which one should I believe and why should I believe it?

Agnosticism—"I don't know"—as an answer describing the actual state of our belief is itself problematic. For *something* happens at death. If we simply cease to exist, we need not worry about the consequences to ourselves after death. Let's make it personal. Something is going to happen to *me*. If I am to be resurrected or reincarnated, and if— as many religions teach—my life on earth has something to do with my happiness (or lack thereof) beyond death, then I cannot escape the issue. I may not know as I wish I could know. But whatever I believe or think I know is either the case or not. My agnosticism—my refusal to wrestle with my doubt until it is resolved—may cost me dearly in the future.

In the final analysis, the question of belief cannot be sidestepped. Why *should* one believe in resurrection or reincarnation or extinction or a ghostly life in a shadowy existence on the Other Side? Why *should* one believe anything at all?

Trading Places

One way to look at belief is to see it along two spectra: a horizontal spectrum from specific to vague and a vertical spectrum from doubtful to certain.

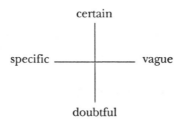

Any person's belief can be plotted on this chart. For example, with regard to the tough questions such as the existence of God, the meaning of life, where are you on the chart? If you have been a member of a close-knit community in which these questions were raised and certain answers were expected, you will probably have many specific beliefs.

Take Jane and Frank. Jane is a college student raised in a traditional Catholic family. Her parents attended church regularly; she attended St. Catherine's, a parochial school in her community, and most of her friends did so as well. She went to confirmation class and, not being a rebellious type, found herself accepting the teachings of the church. When the time came, she was confirmed. She liked her teachers and even considered joining the religious order to which many of them belonged. So she read some manuals designed for those considering the life of a religious. By the time she graduated from high school, however, she had largely abandoned the idea of becoming a nun. Not that she had any doubts about her faith. In fact, at graduation Jane was in the far left and upper quadrant of this chart: specific and certain.

Frank was raised in the same community, but his parents did not attend church, nor did they discuss religion at home. They acknowledged the faith of many of their neighbors, but took a live-and-let-live attitude. Frank's friends were not especially devout as he grew up. He would occasionally wonder if there was a god, but only casually. Actually, Frank's very notion of God was fuzzy, something like the Force in *Star Wars*. For the most part he did not think about religious matters or worry about what would happen after death. None of his friends or close relatives died, so death did not pose itself as a personal threat. He grew up with only vague beliefs about any specifically religious matter. He was not sure there was a god and basically was not interested in finding out. When he graduated from high school, he was firmly in the lower right quadrant of the chart: vague and uncertain.

Both Jane and Frank went to Hansom State University, and both began to change. Jane discovered that she was the lone serious Catholic on her dorm floor. She had joined the youth group from her church in a prolife rally, but at college she found only one other young woman who was prolife or even considered chastity a virtue. She was shaken to the roots. She knew of no other way of life but the one she'd been raised in, and now she began to doubt it. How could so many people her own age believe so many things she didn't? Even the priest at the Newman Center would not take a firm stand on abortion and chastity. She knew only one way to believe, but she had lost all her assurance. By the end of the first semester, she had moved from the upper left quadrant to the quadrant directly below: specific but uncertain. Then during the year that followed, she lost most of her interest in her former Catholic belief; no interest in any other religious or philosophic system replaced it. She was slipping quietly from the lower left to the lower right quadrant: vague and uncertain.

Frank was also profoundly affected by his fellow students. His roommate had been doing yoga meditation in high school. Frank quickly became fascinated, and by the end of the first semester he not only was meditating but had joined a community of students who were privately being taught Eastern philosophy by a college professor who, though American, had studied in Japan for ten years and become a Buddhist priest. Frank had moved from the lower right quadrant first to the lower left quadrant, then quickly to the upper left: specific and certain.

In effect, Frank and Jane had traded places. College is a volatile time, and belief, especially among students, is mobile. Here today, somewhere else tomorrow. Sometimes this mobility is accompanied by great stress and anguish, sometimes not.

Happy Hedonism and Anguished Despair

Frank and Jane are fictional. Sean and Greta, two students I met in Ireland after a lecture on this topic at Ulster University—Jordanstown, are very real.[9] Our conversations went like this.

"You say you can't prove the existence of God. Is that right?" Sean asked.

"Yes, I can't prove with philosophic certitude that God exists. Of course, he either does or doesn't. It's just that I can't *prove* he does the same way I can *prove* that Belfast exists."

"Okay then. So I don't have to believe that he does. I can do whatever I want. Right?"

"Well, not really. If he exists as the Bible says he does, then it would be disastrous not to admit that and recognize his claim on your life. You can't avoid the issue simply by realizing that *proof* of his existence is not so compelling that only an idiot would miss it. If he exists, you are responsible to him. As I tried to show in the lecture, there are many good reasons for believing that God exists and that Jesus has provided our best glimpse of just who he is. The case for the Christian faith is quite strong, so strong that if you miss seeing it to be true, and it turns out to be so, then you will justifiably be held responsible for not seeing it."

"Yes, but you can't prove it, right? That's what you're saying, right? So I can do anything I want, can't I?"

I again explained that I could not *prove* in any rigorous way that God exists but that I had shown him where to go to get the information that would make his own decision an intelligent one. (I had pointed him to the best reason of all—Jesus—as he is shown to be in the Gospels.) But he demanded what no apologist for the Christian faith can provide—a proof then and there that God exists, a proof that required nothing more from him than to listen and to see the conclusion as impossible to miss. So the dialogue never progressed beyond this point. It became obvious that Sean wanted off the hook. He wanted me to say that because I could not prove God to him, he was not obligated to believe anything at all about God and could live as he wanted.

What a difference between Sean and Greta! Greta was patient; she listened through this long, frustrating discussion, waited until Sean had left and then asked, "You say that if God doesn't exist, then human life really doesn't have a purpose, right?"

"Yes, in short, though there is much more to the point."

"Well, I was wondering, why couldn't we just make up our own meaning? Why do we need God?"

"We need a standard outside ourselves," I replied. "Otherwise each of us in making up our own meaning will get in each other's way. Who or what will judge between us when my meaning is to make lots of money at your expense? Or your meaning as a teacher comes from performing psychological experiments on my children while they are in your care at school?"

"Oh," she said. "Yes, I see that. Well, what about . . . ?" I do not remember the details of this conversation. I do remember that I met each of her suggestions with a quite basic rejoinder. Each time she immediately saw the point and raised another objection. It did not take her long to run out of objections. Each time she became more visibly sad, until tears were welling up in her eyes. She saw that without God there is no meaning to life, but she could not believe that he existed or had an answer to her longing for significance.

Here we have paired opposites: Sean the happy, thoughtless hedonist; Greta the anguished, intellectual nihilist. Sean delighted that he now feels justified to be on his own; Greta profoundly disturbed to be facing a universe where she is left alone to make meaning that is finally meaningless.

Testing Your Belief

It's time to take stock. Throughout this book, I will be asking you the reader to do this. If I am right, the issue of belief is not one we can deal with lightly. If we are at all serious about life and its meaning, *our* life and its value, then we will have to think long and hard about who, what and why we believe. So may I suggest you take stock at this point by pondering these questions:

1. Where are you now on the four-quadrant chart?

2. Have you always been there? What did you believe when you first realized that you believed something?

3. Have you changed in either the specific beliefs or the intensity with which you believe?

4. Why have you changed?

5. List all the reasons you can give for why you believe what you believe.

I do not want to badger anyone who is gracious enough to read what I write. But let me add this: If you complete this exercise now, you will be in a much better position to grapple with the discussion that follows.

I was raised a Christian, Presbyterian, and had some
Catholic influence in my life. So my background is essentially
Christian. However, after a brief stint during my youth (ages
eight to fourteen) of fervent and semifervent churchgoing,
I now do not go to church, although I do celebrate Christmas and
Easter with my family.

I believe that religion is a construct of our enculturation as
human beings and our desire for order in an unreasonable world;
religion and the notion of a god or over-soul or whatever
present us with a means to obtain order.

Taking these things into consideration, I guess that what I
believe cannot be divorced from the fact that I was raised as a
Christian. The possibility of God will always exist for me, mostly
because of my upbringing. But I do not believe he is in any way
responsible for what one does while one is living—that is
purely individual experience and responsibility, and it is amusing
to me that God is supposed to exist and means to police and
absolve us for actions that are our own doing and therefore
our own responsibility.

BRYN MAWR STUDENT, 1989

*   *   *

I can't imagine living without a search for truth, but whether
it involves belief in something after death is different for
different people. I don't know if there is anything after death.
But I do believe in seeking good, improving life on earth and
following the tenets of the major world religions as a living
human being. I do not believe in trying to get others to accept
anyone else's belief system!

CARNEGIE MELLON STUDENT, 1989

Why People
Believe
What They
Believe
───
2

In the last decades of the twentieth century, small, unusual religious groups proved fascinating to Americans. Television brought up close and personal the tragic end of the followers of Jim Jones and David Koresh. As the flames leaped high, TV viewers gasped as the final fate of unknown numbers of Branch Davidians—men, women and children—unfolded on their screens.

Then came the question in every viewer's mind. Why? Why did David Koresh's followers believe so firmly that they were among God's elect? Why did they not heed the warnings of the federal officials? And why did they have such strange beliefs about whom God favored and why?

We are interested finally in why we *should* believe what we believe. But it will be helpful if we look first at how we come to have the beliefs that govern our lives.

What follows here is predicated on responses from students at over a hundred universities during the past twelve years. I have not kept records of all of these responses, but I have found the same sorts of responses from a wide variety of student groups. Essentially these responses fall into four categories, with some overlapping: sociological, psychological, religious and philosophical. Occasionally a response will fall outside any of these categories and must be considered separately. We will examine one of these.

In my lecture/discussions on this topic, I ask three questions. The first two are thought questions: (1) Where are you on the belief chart (see page 22)? (2) What reasons can you give yourself for being where you are? I give participants some time to ponder these questions privately. Then I ask, (3) Why *do* people believe what they do? I put participants' answers on a chalkboard under the four categories just noted. Here are the sorts of answers that are given.[1]

Sociological Reasons
I give these answers in a common grammatical and personal form. Obviously, they are expressed in a variety of ways. Here, as in the lecture, the letter X will indicate whatever it is that people believe. X stands for any religious belief or denial thereof: Buddhism, Islam, Branch Davidianism, ad infinitum.

1. My parents believe X. Therefore I believe X.

"My parents" is the most frequently given first answer to the question, Why do people believe what they believe? I am sure this is not just because parents' belief is a major factor, but also because when students reflect on what has influenced them, this is their first thought.

> Beliefs held by the individual and reinforced by the community give one a conceptual framework into which one can place both the everyday and the extraordinary occurrences of life, giving them meaning and significance. (Oberlin, 1991)

2. My friends believe X.

This is the second most frequent answer. Peer pressure, wanting to be like one's friends or the in crowd, is clearly an important factor in molding beliefs.

3. My society believes X.

Society itself, the full social context of one's life, is also mentioned quite frequently. The following comment sums up the first three reasons:

I believe in the "traditional" explanation for who we are, why we're here, what will give us the happiness we all strive for. At first I believed so simply because I was reared in a very strict, very conservative Christian home, educated in a Christian elementary school, and had been going to church on Sundays for as long as I can remember. (Bryn Mawr, 1989; this student's comment continued as she listed other, more philosophic reasons—see philosophical reason 5 below)

4. My culture in general holds *X*.

Belief systems are synonymous with cultural systems. That is, belief systems provide a cultural framework through which action and communication are intelligible to other members of a common group. It is not a matter of "should" one believe; it is a matter of needing to believe in a worldview in order to live or communicate with others in a group. (Haverford, 1989)

5. *X* is all I know about.

Some students give this reason, though, as we will see in chapter three, they just do not realize that they are aware of alternative ways to view the world.

6. *X* is all I understand.

With the presence of so many alternate religions and views of reality, many students are baffled. They often claim only to understand their own beliefs, and some admit confusion about even them.

7. Communities brainwash people into believing *X*.

In the wake of the Jonestown massacre and the Branch Davidian conflagration, some students think that people, perhaps even they themselves, have been manipulated not so much by a single person such as a "cult leader" but by the communities in which they grew up.

Psychological Reasons
When I ask students why people should believe, by far the largest

percentage of all responses fall in the psychological category. Though the surveys were not taken with any statistical precision and no statistically significant conclusions can be drawn, some of the results are notable. At Oberlin, for example, 68 of 169 responses listed psychological reasons as key reasons for belief; at Yale it was 59 out of 144 responses; at Rose-Hulman 82 out of 163 responses; at Ohio State 45 out of 94. Some students were eloquent in their comments.

1. *X* gives meaning, purpose and direction to my life. It brings order out of chaos. It gives a foundation for hope. It keeps me from committing suicide.

If for no other reason, then believe something just to keep from committing suicide. Life is pain. Anyone who says otherwise is selling something.[2] Belief in *something else* is the only feasible alternative to a Camus-response: end it all. (Behrend, 1989)

Because belief is the only thing that can give our existence any meaning; without belief there is nothing preventing us from suicide. And anybody who "truly believes" in existentialism and yet wakes up and goes through each day is a liar, because if they were actually serious they would have let themselves die off anyway. Sartre and Camus's unspoken "belief" was the belief that they were right, and that it was their destiny to show the world how things were, and so basically all of that was a sham, and they believed just as strongly as all of any of us. (Amherst, 1991)

To believe in something in my opinion means to hope. Nothing will ever be perfect for everyone, but you can at least hope for world peace or to end hunger and homelessness in the world. You should believe in yourself and your dreams so that you can help others and still be happy yourself. (Ohio State, 1991)

2. *X* gives me a sense of identity.

People should espouse certain belief systems in order to establish some degree of identity for themselves. Also, having certain beliefs will serve as a guide for making decisions in life. (Bryn Mawr, 1989)

3. *X* relieves guilt and the fear of a future in hell; it gives me a sense of peace.

[Belief] gives people security to believe that someone or something is watching them, and that after they die there will be something waiting for them. Being atheistic/agnostic is a scary thing. (Kenyon, 1991)

People have an instinctive fear of the unknown and a need to understand the world to avoid those fears. That is why, I believe, religions started. People needed to understand why we are here, so they made up mythologies as answers. Belief is more important to avoid fear of the unknown than knowledge, because no one person can know everything, and the big questions like "Why are we here?" "What is life?" remain unanswered. It is easier to accept a religious idea or scientific idea or theory than to accept the fact that no one knows. People need to believe in things to avoid admitting that no one knows, because, like being in the dark, it is too frightening to admit that you don't know what's out there. (Hunter, 1989)

4. *X* makes me feel good.

Generic thought: All beliefs are subjective; one should believe only what makes one feel good. What is true for oneself is what makes one feel good, and that is what one *should* believe, if anything. (Bryn Mawr, 1989)

5. *X* is a crutch for those who can't stand reality.

There isn't a reason. Religion is the crutch for the weak. (Rose-Hulman, 1993)

Postmodern Psychological Reasons
Within the general category of psychological reasons, there are two related reasons that some students give for belief. They are both difficult to understand and to assess.

1. One should believe only what one wants to believe.

I think people have a right to believe whatever they want—be it there is a God or not. (Trinity—Hartford, 1992)

I think people should believe what they like. (Williams, 1991)

2. One should believe in order for anything to exist, including the believer.

If I don't believe anything, then I basically don't exist. (Oberlin, 1991)

Anything wouldn't be anything if no one believed in it. (Oberlin, 1991)

If you don't believe in anything, nothing will be. (Illinois Wesleyan, 1992)

If I cease to believe in existence, I will cease to exist. (University of Michigan—Dearborn, 1991)

I call both of these reasons "postmodern" because they would not likely have been given a hundred years ago. These reasons emphasize the ultimately personal and individualistic nature of much cutting-edge thinking. I can believe anything I want to. There is nothing there for me to believe in before I believe it.

Religious Reasons

There is an oddness about this category. I would expect students to list religious reasons for belief as among their first responses. Surely Christians would refer to the Bible or the church or their pastor. The fact is that sometimes I have to prod them to produce even one. Still, when they see what they have omitted, they give the following as reasons.

1. My pastor/guru/religious authority figure told me. I read it in a book (Bible/Qur'an/Rig Vedas).

Because the prophets, Bible and supernatural miracles all back up God's existence. (Behrend, 1989)

Because as a *Muslim* I am bound to believe certain things without questioning. (Oberlin, 1991)

2. Miracles prove the truth of *X*.

Things happen to people that can only be explained by supernatural reasons. (Bradley, 1992)

3. I have a direct experience of God.

Because Jesus is alive and living in me! (Illinois Wesleyan, 1992)

4. I have had a profoundly deep religious experience.

I believe in God because I know He exists. I have and am experiencing what Jesus Christ can offer. He takes care of me like nobody else can. He loves me beyond [what] any human love can. I know Jesus Christ is the only way because I had been a Buddhist for eighteen years, and what Jesus did and is doing for [me] Buddha could not have done. Besides, there is no historical account of Buddha being resurrected. (Southern Illinois, 1990)

Philosophical Reasons
Occasionally in the lecture/discussion format a philosophical reason will be among the first ones offered by students. Generally, however, such reasons emerge after a number of sociological and psychological reasons are given. On the surveys, philosophical reasons, though never in the majority, are often thoughtfully and occasionally eloquently expressed.
1. *X* is true.
Because it's true!! (Amherst, 1991)
   Whether we like it or not, we base our lives on beliefs. We are presented with many alternatives, and our beliefs must play an important part in which paths we choose. But beyond a "passive belief," beyond an acceptance of whatever beliefs our society, our environment, our friends might program into us, we must *actively* seek Truth and find good reasons for our belief. For the beliefs programmed into us are likely to be incomplete and misleading. (Williams, 1991)
2. *X* is reasonable.
It is important to believe something in order to be able to personalize, categorize, concretize, rationalize all randomness of the world. However, this is not a justification for clutching on to blind faith in order to avoid thinking at all. What we believe must be governed by the fruits of our *own* introspection, and not the influence of our parents, friends and society. We must use what we have—the power to draw logical inferences from what we see around us, and not rely on age-old formulas to tell us what to think! (Yale, 1992)

The universe is too ordered to have happened by "chance" or evolution. It had to have been created by a loving, omnipotent God. (College of the Ozarks, 1991)

3. *X* is logical.

It seems logical. (Kenyon, 1991)

4. There is empirical evidence for *X*.

You should believe that which has empirical validation. And that is all. (Kenyon, 1991)

I don't know much about it, but if there is any factual proof, [for example] from archaeology or what not, then maybe we/I should believe, but I don't know any, so I don't believe. (Amherst, 1991)

We should believe anything at all if we see, hear or experience evidence of it, or if a very credible source tells us. (North Carolina—Chapel Hill, 1991)

Nothing should be believed unless it can be substantiated by one of the five senses. (Ohio State, 1991)

5. I have experienced *X*.

This reason is identical to reason 3 in the religious category. It appears here because "experience" is a subcategory of "evidence" worthy of being considered philosophic as well as religious.

I think people believe things because they appear to be true. So in each person's mind they don't just believe but they *know* God has given each one of us the capacity to know him and thus we have an in-built desire to know him and to know the truth. This is what drives us to seek after him (this and the "thing" that is missing in us, that is the cause of our emptiness until we come into a relationship with him). (Ohio State, 1991)

6. *X* gives the best explanation for the tough issues of life.

Among the surveys there is no response quite like this one. It is, however, the response that incorporates all of the philosophic reasons into one giant reason. The word *best* carries heavy freight, as will be seen in chapter six. One student did catch something of this reason in the comment that follows. It is the remainder of the comment begun in sociological reason 3 (above).

Now I believe [in Christianity] because I have listened to many discussions and debates, thought through many apparent contradictions (e.g., why there is suffering if God is a benevolent deity?) and have historical evidence to back my beliefs. I know I will never have all the answers because my capacities are limited, but through faith I can try my best to live according to my faith, namely God's will for my life. (Bryn Mawr, 1989)

A Biological Reason
There is one more reason for belief that does not fit into any of the above categories. It focuses on the biological dimension of thought. One student expressed it very briefly.

[Belief] is a biological mechanism for the survival of the human race. (Yale, 1992)

Another student took much longer to say the same thing.

The way I see it, one cannot give a reason for believing something, only rationalizations. What a person believes is a function of the structure, the neural structure, of the brain, particularly as it has been determined by the summation of his experience. To give a reason is to attempt to justify the particular brain structure/ego one has. I believe (or rather, when I translate the structure of my brain that arises in the context of considering "why should . . . at all?") I end up saying/objectifying: I believe what one believes is what one feels one needs to believe in order to live efficiently—that is, with the greatest gain with least energy input. (Behrend, 1989)

We will be weighing the merits of the other reasons in the following chapters. But this reason can be dealt with now.

In short, if the explanation these students give is right—belief is a biological function that serves human survival—then belief has been reduced to its utter biological practicality. Either of two results follows. One possibility is that belief in general is a pure biological function without relation to the question why one should believe one thing rather than another. In this case it has nothing to say about *why* one should believe whatever it is that one believes.

Another possibility is that an individual human being's own specific belief is simply a biological function. One believes that one is rational, that one's thought and deliberation can lead to free decisions as an agent. But the fact is that this belief in rationality is itself not only biologically based but biologically determined. In this case rationality is an illusion. There are no real rational reasons for belief and no foundation for answering the question, Why *should* a person believe one thing rather than another?

Naturalistic explanations for human behavior—whether the behavior of our thinking minds or of our will—reduce the rational to the nonrational. It is very bad news indeed if it should be the case that our beliefs are merely a biological mechanism for the survival of the human race. It reduces our longing for meaning and significance, our hope and delight in our rational faculties, to illusion. It even moots the argument for belief's being a biological mechanism. For if it is such a mechanism, then the argument concluding that it is such a mechanism is itself merely a mechanism. There is therefore no good reason to believe that belief is a mere mechanism.[3]

If there is another explanation for why we believe that deals with all the evidence—including the seeming rationality of our revulsion at being reduced to biological robots—then it should have a large claim on being considered correct, and the biological explanation should then be considered at least incomplete if not incorrect.

A Panorama of Possible Positions

This panoramic sweep, these twenty-five reasons, gives a fair picture of how students respond to the question, Why do people believe what they believe? I think the list that emerges in dialogue is not only fair to what they think but equally fair to the facts. We come to believe and continue to believe for a variety of reasons. Many of us—and that includes me—can find a number of reasons among the above that have influenced our belief. My parents, my background as a boy on a Nebraska ranch, the religious and philosophic books I have read, the evidence I have examined as I have pondered this issue over the past forty-plus years—all of these factors and more have been at work. The question is, however, whether any of these reasons are *good* reasons. So my parents were Christians. How much positive weight does that carry? Or is it really a disadvantage? So I studied philosophy and weighed some evidence. How important is that? So I felt the guilt of my sin eased by the forgiveness of Jesus Christ. Is that really a good reason? We will deal directly with this issue in the next four chapters.

I believe in the "traditional" explanation for who we are,
why we're here, what will give us the happiness we all strive for.
At first I believed so simply because I was reared in a very strict,
very conservative Christian home, educated in a Christian
elementary school, and had been going to church on Sundays
for as long as I can remember.

BRYN MAWR STUDENT, 1989

* * *

Belief systems are synonymous with cultural systems.
That is, belief systems provide a cultural framework through
which action and communication are intelligible to other
members of a common group. It is not a matter of "should" one
believe; it is a matter of needing to believe in a worldview in
order to live or communicate with others in a group.

HAVERFORD STUDENT, 1989

The
Social
Context

3

T here is no question that our social background sets the context for all that we do and think. Society and our culture in general are the air we breathe. We can just as much live without the influence of culture's ubiquitous presence as fish can live without water.

When we reflect on why we have come to believe what we believe, the first thing that comes to mind is our parents and our family. Students are right to point this out, as they quickly do when asked to reflect on why they believe.

In a large measure we are who we were fashioned to be by our heritage and our culture. We never knew ourselves to be ourselves until who we were had been set by nature (our specific development of the DNA that governed our growth) and shaped by nurture. We did not choose to believe the things we first believed; we simply came to believe them. Then one day, when our mental and psychological systems had developed sufficiently, we understood ourselves to be ourselves.

A Young Rancher's Belief

Sometime at, say, age four or five, I became aware that I was me. I was not the baby nurtured within the tight-knit family unit where I simply moved and thought and acted consciously but unselfconsciously. I was different. I was unique. I had, of course, been different, unique, all along. I just hadn't recognized it. Then I did.

Still, even then the notion that I believed things never occurred to me. I believed automatically. I learned from my parents, from my grandparents who lived with us, from my teachers and fellow students at the one-room country school I attended, from my growing sensitivity to and love for the river we lived on, the hills above the house and the trees that surrounded us. I believed lots of things. I just didn't know it.

I had a couple of slightly "mystical" experiences. Once I was frightened by three huge thunderheads that rose quickly from the horizon and seemed to pursue me as I rode home, driving the milk cows back to the ranch. Mother had been teaching me privately with some Sunday-school materials she had gotten from her brother's family. I felt myself pursued by the Father, the Son and the Holy Ghost. We called the Holy Spirit the Holy Ghost in those days, and he was just a mite bit frightening!

And one Sunday afternoon during prayer at a church service held in a country schoolhouse, I felt the presence of something odd and looked up to see if there were tongues of fire or perhaps angels hovering above the heads of those who were communing with God.

I didn't know that I believed anything or that it was important to know what one believes and why. I just believed and wondered all unselfconsciously. Then one summer we moved to a small town nearby. I had just finished sixth grade at the country school. The church my parents attended stood across the street from our new house. I learned then about belief, not just what I was supposed to believe but the fact that it was *belief.* Some people, I learned, did not believe what I believed. Whatever my specific belief was, then, was not necessary. I could believe something more and something else. In other words, I was on my own as far as future belief was concerned. I was becoming an adult, at least in part because I was becoming aware of my own responsibility for what I believed. Moreover, from what I was picking up from the pastor of our church, if I believed what I was supposed to believe, it would make a difference in how I lived.

My church did not have confirmation classes as such, but I was beginning to learn and coming to accept the sorts of things that confirmation classes teach—the traditional doctrines of the Christian faith. I knew that I was doing this freely, that I was not being forced. For a while I even resisted making the kind of commitment that is required if one really believes the Christian teachings. But for me the issue was never whether the Christian teachings were true. I had no doubt they were. Instead the issue was, Would I be willing to live by the demands of the Christian teachings? I decided to do this a few weeks into the summer.

The Power of Culture

I recount this story not to focus on my own social context as such, but to illustrate several important points.

First, each of us is limited in our religious options by our childhood environment. I could never have grown up a Hindu. No, not a Hindu, not a Buddhist, not even a believer in a Native American religion. Though there were Indian reservations not far from our ranch, my family never once set foot on one of them—so far as I know. In my society I could have been a Catholic (nominal or active), a Protestant (nominal or active), a not-very-religious-in-particular secularist. But that's about all. Any exposure to any other religious alternatives was limited to pictures and discussions of other cultures in *National Geographic,* to which my parents subscribed.

Second, we first believe without knowing that we are believing. When we discover that we believe, our belief already is laden with specific content. When I discovered that I believed something, I discovered that I believed in Triune God—Father, Son and Holy Spirit— who had created the universe. I believed that Jesus was the Son of

God—not that I grasped much of what that meant. I believed that I was responsible to God for what I did. At least that much was already present at, say, age twelve. After that I was aware of many developments, shifts and changes of belief. I had become self-conscious about my beliefs.

Third, when we learn that we are believing, we become responsible for what we believe. We can no longer shift to our parents or our background the blame for any of our inappropriate beliefs. Nor can we blame our society; we know of too many other societies not like our own. More broadly yet, the more we become aware of the options of other cultures, the less we can say to ourselves or anyone, "I didn't know there was any other way to think about this subject." Today, most students in most universities around the world are well aware that there are multiple ways to deal with the tough issues of life: Is there a God? Who or what is he/she/it? What happens at death? What is the meaning of our sojourn on earth?

The Specific Reasons Evaluated
If what I have said above is a fair picture of our stance as human beings in the world, then what are we to make of the sociological reasons given in chapter two? Are any of these reasons "good" reasons? That is, do these reasons actually justify our believing what we do?

For our purposes, let us set the standard for "good" reasons at the highest level. And let's make it personal. Let's ask: If upon reflection the only reason you could give yourself for believing what you believe were this specific reason, would you be justified in continuing to hold the belief? That is, if the only reason for believing X were that your parents believe(d) X, would that be a good enough reason for you to be justified in continuing to believe X? We will deal with this and the other reasons in turn.

My parents believe X. In dialogues with students, at least in the Western world, this reason is almost universally rejected as inadequate. In fact, the zest with which this rejection is expressed would send chills up their parents' spines. When occasionally someone will say it's a good reason, inevitably he or she proves to be a parent. Still, how many parents will say that *they* are justified in believing what they believe because of their own parents? In the West's individualist societies, few indeed will base their beliefs solely on the fact that their parents believed.

Why are parents so easily rejected as a foundation? Two reasons are quickly given: (1) my beliefs should be *my* beliefs, and (2) my parents could be wrong. I will deal with the first below, under the category of personal or psychological reasons. The second will be examined here.

"If your parents were right, would that be a good reason for belief?" I ask students. The reply is guarded: "Yes, but it would be because it is right, not because it is my parents." Then they often add, "It still has to be my belief, not theirs." I agree on both counts.

My friends believe X. If our parents could be wrong, so could our friends, our next closest set of associations.

My society believes X. If our parents and friends could be wrong, so could our society. Small groups of people bonded by shared values could be wrong. Think of the Branch Davidians. Larger groups could be wrong. Think of the Nazis. Vast numbers of people agreeing on the direction they seek for their world can be wrong. The dominant society of the American South (and much of the North, too) has been wrong about the superiority of the white race.

This puts us as individuals in an awkward position. Each of us is necessarily a member of a family; we find ourselves having chosen friends; we live in intimate terms with others in our society. We can't do otherwise. As a student from Oberlin wrote, "Beliefs held by the individual and reinforced by the community give one a conceptual framework into which one can place both the everyday and the extraordinary occurrences of life, giving them meaning and significance." Very few people have the strength of ego and character to be the perpetual rebel—to stand against their society. Those who do become countercultural usually seek out others like them and form groups, communities or subcultures that reinforce their countercultural values.

The point is, however, that neither the larger society nor the sub-culture can in itself justify our beliefs. For that we have to seek elsewhere.

My culture in general holds X. Even entire cultures can be under-girded by conceptions that are in essential error about essential matters. Primal cultures, for example, hold basically to the notion of a personal spirit that pervades all things—visible and invisible. Traditional Western culture from the Middle Ages to the Enlightenment held to the notion of a Creator God to whom all people were responsible. Secular Western culture of the past two centuries or so holds that there is no such personal spirit—or any spirit at all—inherent in nature. In fact, traditional cultures of all sorts—Chinese, Indian, Western Enlightenment—maintained firm patterns of beliefs, each of which contradicted those of other cultures. Some of these patterns of beliefs, or aspects thereof, must therefore necessarily be wrong.

Modern world culture, experiencing the breakup of Enlightenment confidence in human reason and witnessing the emergence of post-modernism, is individualistic, pluralistic and culturally relativistic; almost any thought or action is allowable; all standards, all values are equal. I who write and most of you who read this book live in this modern world culture. We have open to us a vast panorama of mutually conflicting values, dreams, agendas, hopes, aspirations. None of us can rely on our culture to justify our beliefs. Our chaotic culture justifies any and all beliefs, thereby justifying none of them. It is our chaotic culture that needs, but in its present state will never get, justification.

X is all I know about. This is just counterfactual, at least for all university students and all—or almost all—readers of this book. Who of us can say we know of only one view of God, death, human responsibility or human meaning? In modern societies only children could not know about religious beliefs other than those of their immediate society. In tightly knit tribal societies some adults would know only about the beliefs of their tribe, but as time passes there are fewer and fewer of these. Those who actually do not know *about* alternatives to their beliefs may be at least epistemically justified in believing the only things they know to believe.[1] The point here is that, except for children, there are very few people in this condition in the modern world.

X is all I understand. Many of us are in this condition. We may dwell in the left half of the belief chart (see page 22) and be vague about our beliefs, but when we reflect, at least we can identify some of them. It's the other options we don't grasp. Many who believe in reincarnation or annihilation have never seriously conceived in the possibility of resurrection, and vice versa. In the "modern world culture" it is becoming more and more necessary that we learn in some detail what we only perceive in vague outline. Our ignorance will neither justify our beliefs nor be an excuse for our errors in belief. The good news is that we do not need to be ignorant. Ignorance is a curable disease. The bad news is that it takes effort. The good news, again, is that our effort will be rewarded.

Communities brainwash people into believing X. If this is the case with any given person in any given community, then, of course, it is a utterly inadequate as a justification for belief. It is in fact a good reason to reevaluate the belief totally afresh. The word *brainwash,* of course, is hardly a technical term and has been rejected by the psychological community. Psychologists would prefer to speak of *coercive persuasion,* a term used to identify a variety of techniques for manipulating belief and behavior. It is not necessary to decide how or even whether these techniques work. We need only note that if they do, they ought not be used. They violate the human right to think clearly about what one should believe and the concomitant right to follow freely the direction that seems most likely to be true.

Reasons and Causes

As we reflect on these seven factors, something should dawn on us. Every one of them is a *cause* that brings about belief. None of them is a *reason* for believing. This is an important distinction and needs to be understood.[2]

I am using the term *cause* to identify a factor over which we are not exercising conscious, rational control. We were caused to be born through no choice of our own. There was nothing we could do about it. Christian values, ideas and norms were instilled into me before I knew it. I was caused to be essentially Christian in my moral and intellectual orientation. An Indian child born to a Hindu family in Poona, all things being normal, becomes a Hindu before she knows it. She is caused to be essentially Hindu. What we find ourselves to be when we come to full intellectual and moral self-consciousness has not been a matter of our self-conscious reflection but a matter of our socialization.

In other words, *causes* act on us without passing through our self-conscious cognitive faculties. This is not to say that we have been utterly determined; it is to say that much about us—much very important about us—is determined not by us but by others. It is not that we have not thought about our beliefs; it is rather that the way we use our minds has been so shaped by our social environment that we are not yet conscious of what has happened to us. Eventually, as we mature, we will become responsible for what we believe. It is reasons that come into play at that point.

A *reason* is a rational justification for our belief. *Reasons* enter the picture when we become old enough to be intellectually and morally aware. We then become responsible for what we do with what we know or think we know, what we believe when we become aware that we believe.

Many American children are *caused* to believe in Santa Claus. But they would not be justified in clinging to this belief after they discovered their parents filling their stockings late Christmas Eve. They would in such a case have a reason for believing that Santa Claus is only a myth.

Likewise, many Christians believe that Jesus died and rose bodily from the dead because they were taught this by their parents and by their church. There may be very good *reasons* for believing their parents or their church, but in a skeptical and pluralistic age like ours (in which so many people believe Jesus did not rise from the dead), those reasons must be more than the fact that one was raised in a Christian social context. One must face not only face the question, Why *do* you believe in the resurrection? but the tougher question, Why, in light of so much rejection of this belief in the surrounding society, *should* you believe this? Are you justified in believing what seems so odd, so magical, so "impossible" in light of what we think we know about return to life after death?

Another way to see the distinction between causes and reasons is to note that *causes* are factors outside our control and *reasons* are those factors that we recognize as rational justifications for our beliefs.

So here we are, people formed and shaped by factors over which we have no control, yet moral agents responsible for our beliefs. Sociological factors are only causes. As thoughtful adults, we will find no justification for our beliefs there. Maybe psychology can help us.

Well, I think because in order to live yourself, and to believe
in yourself so you can believe in other people and help them;
so you can live and enjoy your life, you need to believe in
something. Whatever it may be.

BRYN MAWR STUDENT, 1989

*   *   *

Because if you don't believe in something or someone,
it is impossible to believe in yourself. And believing in yourself
is the best reason to live.

BUCKNELL STUDENT, 1990

*   *   *

If there was nothing to believe in, then life wouldn't really have
a point. There would be no values or morals—the
basic structure of our society.

HUNTER STUDENT, 1989

———————

The
Personal
Context

4

One thread runs through many students' responses to "Why should anyone believe anything at all?" *Belief must be personal. I must be the one to decide.* One could paraphrase the old spiritual:
Not my father, not my mother, but it's me,
Whoever or whatever is up there or out there (if anyone),
Sittin' in the driver's seat.
If you need to believe something, and we all do, then let it be each person's decision. Make it up, if you have to or want to. It's your business. As the student at Bryn Mawr said, "You need to believe in something. Whatever it may be."

The Postmodern Condition of Belief
Though in chapter two I listed general psychological reasons before postmodern psychological reasons, here I would like to reverse the order. The postmodern reasons are profoundly personal, and they reveal why the general psychological reasons are so numerous. They

sum up the essence of every psychological reason. We will start with the more common of the two.

One should believe only what one wants to believe. Expressed in a variety of ways, this reason touches the heart of the matter. People do not wish to have any particular belief imposed on them. "I think people should believe what they like," said one Williams College student. "I think people have a right to believe whatever they want—be it there is a God or not," a Trinity College—Hartford student put it.

In one sense these remarks are correct. No one's belief should be imposed—that is, forced—on someone else. In matters of basic orientation to God, each other and the universe, we are and ought to be free to believe for ourselves. Manipulation—coercive persuasion— is an invasion of a person's soul.

Moreover, each person's belief must be the belief of that person. It can't be someone else's, as if one could turn over one's whole mind as well as will to another's belief. It can't be done and shouldn't be tried.

With these two issues, however, what we have are *necessary conditions,* not *sufficient reasons.* That is, a person's belief must be freely acknowledged and held, and it must be his or her own. That is a moral right (and should be a legal right as well). But freedom to believe what one takes to be true is no justification for believing any specific thing.[1]

Still, I am confident, because of many extensive conversations with students, that more is being intended by the "believe-what-you-want" comments than such necessary conditions. What lies just below the surface is the human desire for autonomy. We all want things to be just as we want them to be.

In a survey at Michigan State University, students were asked, "Do you believe there is a G(g)od? If so, what do you think this God is like?" One student answered, "God is everything each person thinks of him/her." In similar survey at Haverford College, another student wrote,

> God exists in each individual, and the *form* which their God takes is entirely up to them. To say there is *one* God, or dictate a God or

concept of God to someone other than yourself, is denying them the chance to experience God for themselves, and therefore I think it is unfair. Yes, God exists, but to each his/her own.

Such a "god" becomes a mere psychological category or a subject of one's personality with no objective referent.[2]

When we make up our god, what does he look like? At least forty students at Michigan State limited their description of God solely to those aspects highly favorable to us. God is said to be "all love," "flexible and understanding," "all forgiving," "a very kind man," " a good spirit," "nice" and so on. Missing here was any sense of a God who might be holy or righteous, who might call his creatures to be holy and righteous or hold them responsible for their deeds. God is rather a Cosmic Grandfather, the wimpy god Convenience, the Mush God. These students might all have prefaced their comments as one student did: "I like to think of God as . . ."[3]

But surely, if there is a deity worthy of deity, then he/she/it will not just be what we think of him/her/it. What we "like to think of God as being" is much more likely to be a pure figment of our imagination.

We turn, then, to the more troublesome of the two postmodern reasons.

One should believe in order for anything to exist, including the believer. I suspect that this reason will seem strange to most readers. Only a handful of students make such comments. But out of a hundred responses, regardless of the college where the survey is made, there seem always to be one or two who do. That's enough to ask what's going on here.

These responses take us beyond even the social-construction-of-reality theories of the "modern" sociologists, theories that say that how a culture thinks about reality is socially determined. Here reality is, rather, up to each of us to construct.

In the late twentieth century there are two versions of this view. One is associated with the New Age movement. Shirley MacLaine, for example, emphasizes the creative power and divinity of each person.

MacLaine says that reality is what she makes of it. "I could legitimately say that I created the Statue of Liberty, chocolate chip cookies, the Beatles, terrorism, and the Vietnam War. . . . And if [people] reacted to world events, then I was creating them to react so I would have someone to interact with, thereby enabling me to know myself better."[4]

MacLaine, however, also says it's up to the rest of us to do likewise. We can become our own Higher Selves, our own "gods."[5] Or as John Lilly, another New Age proponent, put it, "All and every thing that one can imagine exists."[6]

This general set of reasons takes a very different form in Richard Rorty's philosophy. MacLaine is a pantheist. Rorty is a naturalist who dismisses the human ability to access the actual physical world. All we have is language. If we can convince others to speak in the same way, tell the same sorts of stories, we have formed the human, social and private world not just for ourselves but for others.[7]

Because of the brevity of the most students' responses, it is impossible to know just what they were intending by their we-create-our-own-reality remarks. Were they just the product of youthful nihilism? How seriously do the students believe they affect reality by their belief? Are they pantheists who somehow believe that they have creative powers because of their essential divinity? (Perhaps some are.) Are they prototypes of postmodern secularists, like Rorty, who are on the cutting edge of modern thought? (It's hard to say.)

In any case, the perspective from which these comments come is growing in adherents—of both a pantheist and a secular type. And in the "popular" form in which they appear here, these views have many campus adherents. The question one must ask is this: Is there any reason to think we are either (1) so powerful as creative human beings that we can actually fashion reality or (2) so lacking in mental ability that all of what we *think* we know about the outer world we *don't* know? The matter demands much more attention than can be given it in this chapter; I will return to it in chapter five. Here I simply note the problematic nature of the claims these reasons make.

Psychological Reasons

When students list single reasons for their belief, as most do in the surveys, the single most frequent reasons given fall in the category of psychology. How strong are the reasons? If these were the only sorts of reasons one had to believe, would any one of these—or all put together—be strong enough to justify one's belief? Sociological "reasons" were found on analysis not to be reasons at all. Is the same true of these reasons?

X gives meaning, purpose and direction to my life. It brings order out of chaos and gives a foundation for hope. It keeps me from committing suicide. This closely related set of reasons is the most frequent form that the psychological reasons take on student surveys. Do beliefs act as students say they do? The answer is clearly yes. Witness the poignancy with which these reasons are sometimes expressed.

If for no other reason, then believe something just to keep from committing suicide. Life is pain. Anyone who says otherwise is selling something. Belief in *something else* is the only feasible alternative to a Camus-response: end it all. (Behrend, 1989)

Because belief is the only thing that can give our existence any meaning; without belief there is nothing preventing us from suicide. And anybody who "truly believes" in existentialism and yet wakes up and goes through each day is a liar, because if they were actually serious they would have let themselves die off anyway. Sartre and Camus's unspoken "belief" was the belief that they were right, and that it was their destiny to show the world how things were, and so basically all of that was a sham, and they believed just as strongly as all of any of us. (Amherst, 1991)

These students know that the answers to the tough issues of life do not come easily, nor are they certain. Why are we here? Are we just an undesigned complex combination of matter with the power of consciousness? Are we sparks of the divine? Are we the creation of a holy and righteous God, responsible to him to be who we were created to be? About such questions something must be *believed,* for utter philosophical certitude cannot be reached.

People deal with these questions in different ways, of course. Some struggle with them till they reach some sort of resolution and find a peace about the answers they are believing; then they get on with life. Others seem to be in perpetual doubt about any answers. Still others, unable to resolve the issues, suppress the questions with endless activity, sports, entertainment, the eternal Walkman, anything to keep from being alone with their own thoughts. For them a "belief" in the value, the security, of the present moment of stimulation becomes ingrained, subconscious.

For the perpetually thoughtful, however, this will not work. The issues are either resolved with confident belief or held in abeyance with constant rumination. Sometimes the rumination is so agonizing that suicide seems to be the only way out.

Camus is worth quoting. His name comes up often in responses from thoughtful students.

There is but one truly serious philosophical problem, and that is suicide. Judging whether life is worth living amounts to answering the fundamental question of philosophy. . . . I see many people die because they judge that life is not worth living. I see others paradoxically getting killed for the ideas or illusions that give them a reason for living (what is called a reason for living is an excellent reason for dying). I therefore conclude that the meaning of life is the most urgent of questions.[8]

Camus tries (unsuccessfully, I think) in the next ninety pages to show how even without God, life can be made meaningful by one's own effort.[9] Essentially Camus's answer, given its best expression in his novel *The Plague*, is to counsel a perpetual, intense affirmation of the value of human life. Our lives are plagued by a universe that does not fit human aspirations; fight against this plague; in the face of certain death with no afterlife, live life to the fullest and fight for the fullest life of your friends, your city, your country, your world. It is a noble call. But it is predicated solely on each individual's intense affirmation of value in an otherwise valueless world.[10]

Camus's philosophy is a philosophy for the brave, for those courageous enough to recognize the meaninglessness of a world in which God is dead, a world of sheer fact. At its best it provides incentive only to the philosophic few with strong egos. To make yourself, to be who you choose to be, to live as you project yourself into the future, knowing that all life ends with physical death, that there is no ground but your own choice for the values you affirm—this is not a philosophy for the ordinary person. It is for those who would be more than ordinary, a philosophy for the Übermensch, Nietzsche's superman. Nietzsche could not sustain even himself in such a role, and spent the last ten years of his life either in a mental institution or being taken care of by his mother and sister.[11] The counsel of Camus and his sometime colleague Jean-Paul Sartre is finally a counsel of temporary hope in a world of final despair. It is found satisfactory only by an elite cadre of the psychologically strong.

Most students, most people, do not carry their ruminations to the depths of Camus. But they do see something of what he sees: we need something to give our lives meaning. Belief can and does give that. Even though we are now having severe difficulty, if we believe that ultimately things are going to work out okay, then we can get through life. This explains, I think, why so many of our pictures of God are drawn with our convenience in mind. If God is "nice" or "all forgiving," and that's all, then I'm home free. I can do anything I want.

The problem is, Is God like that? Or does he judge us on the basis of standards of holiness and righteousness that none of us can rise to? Or is there a God at all?

If the only reason we have for our belief is that it gives us meaning and keeps us from suicide, then we may be deluding ourselves. Is God, is the moral universe, is reality like what we think it is?

Just as our parents, our society and our culture could be wrong about these things, so could we. The question is, What is really the case? Are our beliefs true? Convenience is not an adequate test of objective truth.

X gives me a sense of identity. Beliefs can indeed give me a sense of identity. I can find myself as a part of a larger group, so that I can say, "I'm a Buddhist," or "I'm a Republican," or "I'm a Christian." But what if my belief is misguided or just downright wrong? I still have the identity, but my belief is not justified.

X relieves guilt and the fear of a future in hell; it gives me a sense of peace. Christians especially give this as a reason for belief. It was a major reason for my own conversion.

I believed my pastor when he said that God is holy and requires from each of us a holy life. That squared with what I had picked up living on the ranch. He said that neither I nor anyone else met God's requirements. I could see that for myself. He said that God offers forgiveness for my unrighteousness and explained how to confess my condition to God and accept his forgiveness through what Jesus Christ did in dying in my place. I did not do this upon first hearing. But eventually I did. Indeed, Christianity relieved my feelings of guilt and my fear of death. I was given a sense of peace.

But—and this may be hard for firm Christian believers to accept— we could be wrong. Our experience as such does not fully justify our belief. Some people are relieved by yoga meditation, some by immersing themselves in activity, some by secular therapy.

It may be scary, as one student said, to be an atheist or an agnostic, but scariness is not proof of falsehood. If it were, there would be no terrorists. Sometimes the scary is true.

Nonetheless, there is some evidential value in experience. If something about us is true—for example, that we are sinners in the hands of a merciful God—then we can expect that experience will serve to help confirm this. Though experience is a legitimate part of a cumulative argument, the experience in itself is not sufficient. We will look at this issue again in chapters six and fourteen.

X makes me feel good. This is a very popular way to sum up the psychological reasons: "It makes me feel good; I like it." As one student put it:

> Generic thought: All beliefs are subjective; one should believe only what makes one feel good. What is true for oneself is what makes one feel good, is what one *should* believe, if anything. (Hunter, 1989)

We have already seen the inadequacy of this notion. But it is worth looking at again, this time from its reverse. Should I ever believe something that does *not* make me feel good? Should I ever believe something that brings anxiety instead of peace, brings feelings of guilt rather than forgiveness, challenges my sense of dignity and identity, puts at risk my whole reason for living?

The question hardly needs pondering. Of course there are times when I should believe such things. If a qualified set of doctors tell me with no hesitation that I have cancer, should I believe it? Yes. Does it give me comfort? No! But it's most likely to be true, and only if I believe it is there much chance of being rid of the cancer or of prolonging my life.

There is sometimes a heavy cost to the pursuit of good feelings. A couple of decades ago a drug called thalidomide was prescribed by doctors to women with problem pregnancies, for the relief of morning sickness. It worked—that is, it relieved the discomfort. But it also caused children to be born severely handicapped by underdeveloped arms and legs. The drug was withdrawn from use, of course. Its side effects were too costly.

A belief that makes you feel good may be just as dangerous as thalidomide. If God is not just "nice" but requires from us an acknowledgment of our guilt and our trust in what he has done for us, then we are ultimately in worse shape than a handicapped child. But then we must also say that if God is not merciful, or if his mercy is only accessed through yogalike meditation, or if God is not personally concerned for us and we are reincarnated solely according to our deeds in this life, then even confession and acceptance of Christ could bring us back in the next life more miserable than we are in this one.

The point is what we believe must be true, not just convenient. Truth should be our exclusive aim.

X is a crutch for those who can't stand reality. I have no doubt that this is an explanation for a great deal of belief, especially in the modern world. We are inundated with misery—our own and that of others.

As I write this, cities along the Mississippi and its tributaries in Iowa and Minnesota are flooded, hundreds of houses and businesses are under water, millions of acres of farmland will produce little if any crop this year. In situations like this people fall back on the beliefs that have given them hope, they question the ground of these beliefs, they rely on them to carry them through, or they abandon them and look elsewhere. Some sink into despair. Crutches are very important to people with broken legs. Like crutches to help the injured to walk, beliefs indeed provide support for hope.

The problem with crutches is that some of them do not hold the weight put on them. They break under stress. Beliefs that are not strong enough will not hold us through the agonies of life. Beliefs that are not true will not hold us beyond death.

Experience as a Reason

The psychological factors we have examined above are reasons, not causes. This is vital to note. In essence, *psychological reasons* is another term for *personal experience.*

Personal experience—whether one's own or reports of others'—has an ambivalent value. On the one hand, there is nothing stronger or more compelling than seeing, feeling, hearing, tasting, touching, even smelling for oneself.

Courtship is all about learning by direct involvement. Is she really as beautiful on the inside as on the outside? Is this guy for real? Can I trust him? Will she betray me? What will he be like six months, a year, ten years, fifty years from now? Somehow we believe that what we directly experience over a period of time is the best guide we have to who our best friends really are.

We check our experience against that of our friends. We listen to what they say about the one we are thinking of marrying. We hear their stories, the tales of his involvement with our best friend, the accounts of what she did and said at the parties she went to a year ago. We listen, we experience, we make our decision, and sometimes we make our commitment. Experience *can* be positive evidence for belief.

But there is a negative side as well, a limitation to experience as a judge of a person's character. People put on a front, they deceive us by their words and actions. No amount of experience can take us all the way to philosophical certitude concerning the real character of even our closest friends, our wives or husbands or children. Moreover, we deceive ourselves either by overcaution or by credulity and trusting too much. Sometimes we see only what we want to see. The guy is a crass philanderer, but she sees him as Prince Charming. She's a gold digger, but he loves her fascination with the ins and outs of his business dealings.

Seemingly religious experience does not carry with it its own interpretation.[12] Without a proper frame of reference, data—even the data of personal involvement—can lead one to tragically wrong judgments. Life is a risk. Given all the mistakes we could so easily make, it's amazing that we do as well as we do.

All limitations aside, however, experience—our own and that we hear from others—is still one of the best sources we have for determining the truth of a belief.

Jesus is alive and living in me!

* * *

The prophets, Bible and supernatural miracles all back up
God's existence.

* * *

Things happen to people that can only be explained
by supernatural reasons.

The
Religious
Dimension

5

R eligious reasons for religious beliefs would seem to be the most
obvious to occur to anyone who was asked. I thought, for example, that the Bible would be one of the first things mentioned
by students in North America as a reason for religious belief. It rarely
is mentioned, nor is the Qur'an or even a religious figure like the
pope, Billy Graham or a Zen master.

I can only speculate as to the reason for this. Perhaps it's because
the academic world is so secular, so insistent that religious reasons
have no place in the university. This rubs off on students attending
a philosophic sort of lecture, even one given by a Christian. They may
think it's just passé to mention the Bible or refer to their pastor or
church. When Christians cite the Bible as an authority even in religion classes, they are often ridiculed (usually mildly) by the professor
and other students. So why suffer humiliation by saying the word *Bible*
out loud in a university lecture hall?

Perhaps it does not occur to them that the Bible is in fact a possible reason for belief in the most common religion in North America. So are the religious communities and their leaders. Perhaps they are too unfamiliar with what the Bible and these communities claim to be. In any case, I find it odd.

Religious Reasons

Religious reasons do emerge when I probe for them. Let's examine them to see if any, taken alone, would be a "good" reason for believing—one so strong that it alone could justify one's belief.

My pastor/guru/religious authority figure told me. I read it in a book of scripture [Bible, Qur'an, Rig Veda, Book of Mormon, etc.]. We can combine these two sorts of reasons into one because the same issue is involved in each: authority. People who believe what the scriptures and the religious leaders of their tradition say are relying on the knowledge and wisdom of those people and those ancient texts. They trust the source.

One Muslim student at Oberlin put the matter in the extreme: "As a *Muslim* I am bound to believe certain things without questioning."

Some would say that this is the most foolish thing one can do. We should trust no one and doubt everything. Especially, we should doubt texts that claim to tell us what we could never know on our own—how a god made the world, for example. If you are to trust anyone, let it be yourself. As a student at the University of Chicago said,

I don't think the individual should believe "anything at all"—I think each person should work out his or her own religious beliefs. I believe that God exists, but that no human being can know his will for certain, and therefore we all have the responsibility to follow our own consciences.

So the question is this: What reason is there for accepting any given religious authority? Why should any one be accepted as an authority on anything at all?

When the question is posed in this way, a whole new dimension opens up. We notice immediately that the religious realm is not the only realm that relies on authority. It happens in every field.

We go to doctors when we are ill because we trust them to know a lot about what might ail us. They have studied and practiced for years. They should know. And often they do. What they prescribe is followed by our recovery. That doesn't prove the truth of the doctor's diagnosis and therapy; we might have healed without the healer. But the evidence for the value of following the "doctor's orders" is overwhelming.

We ask physicists about the physical shape of the universe; few of us have any idea how they have arrived at the answers they give. We realize that the subject requires more study and more mathematical ability than most of us have. We trust the community of physicists to weed out the eccentric pseudoscientist who could easily fool most of us.

We accept the authority of the auto mechanic who fixes our cars, the butcher who helps us select the best cut of steak for a special dinner, the librarian who finds the unfindable book for us. In short, we accept authority all the time. And we learn by experience whether the trust we have placed in those authorities has been misplaced.

There is no difference with religious authorities. Does what they say "check out"? Do those religious texts that claim to record historical events do so accurately? How do they square with other documents that attest to events at the same time period? Compare, for example, the extrabiblical data for events recorded in the Bible with the extra-Book-of-Mormon data for events recorded in the Book of Mormon.

Does what the texts or religious experts say square with our experience? How accurate to human nature as we understand it is what is said in the Bible, for example? Is the world really as violent as we find it described in the book of Judges? Or is it more like the reality described in Mary Baker Eddy's *Science and Health with Key to the Scriptures,* the authoritative text of Christian Science?

Is there any reason to think that some religious figures have an insight into who God is and what he wants? Or any reason to trust what a Zen master says about the way to peace? Here each teacher must be examined individually. Some may have far more likelihood of knowing what they are talking about than others. The fact that a teacher has followers points first to popularity, not to reliability. Is there any reason to think that any one or more of them really do have special knowledge?

In the final analysis, we should accept as reliable authority only those texts and people we believe are telling the truth. Truth is the issue, not the source of the truth. The source does not ensure the truth; only the facts of the matter do that. But if the source can be relied on to tell the truth, then we can trust the source. Is there any reason for thinking any text or person does exactly that?

I will return to this reason in chapters seven through ten.

Miracles prove the truth of X. What a muddle this reason is! On the one hand, if an event that appears to be a miracle is in fact a miracle (an event that could not occur without supernatural intervention), then it proves that there is a supernatural dimension. If there are miracles, then there is a supernatural.

On the other hand, how do we know that the event is a miracle? How do we know it could not have occurred by purely natural causes? Moreover, the claim that such events occurred in history—like Jesus' walking on water or rising from the dead—could simply be legend, the pious imaginings of Jesus' naive followers. Why should we trust a text like the Gospel of Mark that recounts many such events? Lots of religions claim supernatural events. So why should the supernatural events of one religion prove that religion while the significance of the supernatural events of other religions is ignored?

Miracles are indeed problematic as proofs of religious beliefs. But they are not to be ignored. As I will try to show in chapters six and eleven, they do have evidential value—just not as much as many people, especially many Christians, think.

I have had a direct experience of God or Ultimate Reality. What could be greater proof for the existence of God than a direct experience of him? William James speaks of the noetic power of mystical experience—heightened states of awareness that we take to be the results of direct contact with the supernatural.

Mystical states seem to those who experience them to be also states of knowledge. They are states of insight into depths of truth unplumbed by the discursive intellect. They are illuminations, revelations, full of significance and importance, all inarticulate though they remain; and as a rule they carry with them a curious sense of authority for after-time.[1]

There is no question that people of many religious traditions have had these sorts of experiences. James documents a wide variety, and the religious sections of bookstores are loaded with accounts of them.[2] The question James raises, and that we must too, is whether these experiences can be counted on to lead us to the truth about the supernatural. In the quotation above, James calls them "states of insight into depths of truth unplumbed by the discursive intellect," but later he questions this, finally giving only a guarded approval of mystical states as insights into truth.[3]

(1) Mystical states, when well developed, usually are, and have the right to be, absolutely authoritative over the individuals to whom they come.

(2) No authority emanates from them which should make it a duty for those who stand outside of them to accept their revelations uncritically.

(3) They break down the authority of the non-mystical or rationalistic consciousness, based upon the understanding and the senses alone. They show it to be only one kind of consciousness. They open out the possibility of other orders of truth, in which, so far as anything in us vitally responds to them, we may freely continue to have faith.[4]

But there is a problem with accepting James's assessment. James holds that those having these experiences are in essential agreement that they have become one with the divine in such a way as to favor pantheism more than a strict theism. But this is not, I think, true. The religious and philosophical content of mystical experiences actually varies widely from person to person. Some who have had mystical experiences point to the distance they feel between them and God even while they detect his presence with them. (I will quote the record of one such experience presently.) And some of the Christian texts James uses to illustrate pantheistic tendencies can be better read in fully nonpantheistic ways.[5] James's bias toward finding commonalities led, I think, to his pantheistic interpretation of the texts of the theistic mystics.[6]

If mystical experiences have the authority James attributes to them, then either one of two things follows: (1) ultimate reality is indeterminate, not even uniform enough to sustain scientific inquiry, or (2) having a mystical experience justifies one in believing something regardless of its truth. If some mystical experiences point to pantheism and others to theism, one of them must be mistaken or misinterpreted.

James tries to get out of this dilemma by saying that the mystical experience is authoritative only to the one who has it. The rest of us can rely on our own experiences or assess critically those of others. Still, that leaves at least some who have these profound experiences justified in believing what must necessarily be untrue.

I think there is another, much better way to assess the noetic quality of religious experience. That is to see it as one very important clue to what really is true. Mystical experiences should not be uncritically accepted as pointing to the truth, even by those who have them. Yes, they have a powerful noetic effect. Yes, they are clues to the truth. No, they are not finally authoritative, even to those who feel that they are.

Before I suggest what this better way is, let us look at two radically different "religious" experiences. The first is one recorded by a famous seventeenth-century scientist.

Pascal and the God of Abraham, Isaac and Jacob

During his brief life, Blaise Pascal (1623-1666), a brilliant mathematician and philosopher, was engaged in two pursuits—science and Christian apologetics. Raised in a family that served the French aristocracy, Pascal was educated privately by his scholarly father. A prodigy at mathematics, he early developed a reputation rivaling that of men like René Descartes, some years his elder. In his twenties he began work on the problem of the vacuum and became involved in a controversy with the Jesuits. In 1646 he and his family became committed Christians and followers of the Jansenist sect (an Augustinian strain of Catholicism). Much of his life was spent in illness and pain. In his late twenties, his "worldly" period, he hobnobbed with court figures and generally tasted as much as he could of the "good life." He is most noted, however, for proving that a vacuum could exist, solving for the first time several puzzling mathematical problems and building the first calculating machine.

In 1654 something dramatic happened that changed the course of his life. Though he never spoke of this experience before his death, he left a record of it sewn into the lining of his coat. These pages were discovered after his death and have become not just an important documentation of Pascal's biography but a classic of the spiritual life of Christians.

The year of grace 1654.

Monday, 23 November, feast of Saint Clement, Pope and Martyr, and of others in the Martyrology.

Eve of Saint Chrysogonus, Martyr and others.

From about half past ten in the evening until half past midnight.

Fire

"God of Abraham, God of Isaac, God of Jacob," not of philosophers and scholars.

Certainty, certainty, heartfelt, joy, peace.

God of Jesus Christ.

God of Jesus Christ.

My God and your God.

"Thy God shall be my God."

The world forgotten, and everything except God.

He can only be found by the ways taught in the Gospels.

Greatness of the human soul.

"O righteous Father, the world has not known thee, but I have known thee."

Joy, joy, joy, tears of joy.

I have cut off myself from him.

They have forsaken me, the fountain of living waters.

"My God wilt thou forsake me?"

Let me not be cut off from him for ever!

"And this is life eternal, that they might know thee, the only true God, and Jesus Christ whom thou has sent."

Jesus Christ.

Jesus Christ.

I have cut myself off from him, shunned him, denied him, crucified him.

Let me never be cut off from him!

He can only be kept by the ways taught in the Gospel.

Sweet and total renunciation.

Total submission to Jesus Christ and my director.

Everlasting joy in return for one day's effort on earth.

I will not forget thy word. Amen.

The first thing to note is that this "memorial" attests to what is clearly a mystical experience. It fits three of James's four criteria: noetic quality, transiency and passivity.[7] The fourth—ineffability—is interesting in both its presence and its absence. "Fire," Pascal wrote. Something about the experience was way beyond description. The word suggests an intensity beyond compare, being wrapped up in an experience so profound that only a metaphor will do, and one senses that even that does not do the experience justice.

Second, this is not a record of a pantheistic experience. Pascal sees a clear distinction between himself and God.

Third, it is an experience of a specific God—a personal God (the God of Abraham, Isaac and Jacob; Jesus Christ and the God of Jesus Christ), not a philosophic abstraction.[8] Though the experience lasted only a couple of hours, it seemed to him timeless. The experience ranged from "fire," to joy, to anguish for his sins and a sense of deserved separation from a holy God, to fear, to total renunciation and back to joy as his experience reached a resolution.

Fourth, Pascal's experience was profoundly *contentful*—one could even say "rational" in that twice he acknowledges a written text, the Bible, as the source of truth about God. What one could do with one's intelligence—read and understand the Scripture—should be done. The work of the mind was not to be abandoned.

This is an intensely rich expression of Pascal's experience. So much more could be observed and said about it. I will make only one last comment: this is an experience of a specific God within a specific tradition that holds to a specific authoritative revelation. The noetic power of this experience served to give Pascal a "certitude" (he repeated the word) that was unshakable.

In answering the question why one should believe in God, Pascal could say to himself if not to us, "I have had a direct experience of God."[9]

William James is loath to consider religious experiences that include sights and sounds as "mystical." But there are as many or more of these in the available literature than there are of the types he does include. And many of them have at least some of the same characteristics—a noetic quality, transience and a rejection of reason alone as a guide to knowing. Take the following experience of Shirley MacLaine.

MacLaine: A Trip Almost to the Moon
Shirley MacLaine, the movie star and nightclub performer, in several biographies recounts many stories of trance experiences. Picture her sitting in a natural sulfur spring spa in a bathhouse high in the Andes Mountains of Peru. There is little light except from a candle. She is being guided in her thoughts and experiences by a friend she calls David. He has her relax in the so-called medicinal waters and stare at the flame of a candle.

I physically felt a kind of tunnel open in my mind. It grew like a cavern of clear space that was open and free of jumble. It didn't feel like thought. It felt actually physical. . . . I became the space in my mind. I felt myself flow into the space, fill it, and float off, rising out of my body until I began to soar. I was aware that my body remained in the water. I looked down and saw it. David stood next to it. My spirit or mind or soul, or whatever it was, climbed higher into space. Right through the ceiling of the pool house and upward over the twilight river I literally felt I was flying. . . . And attached to my spirit was a thin, thin silver cord that remained stretched though attached to my body in the pool of water.[10]

As she soars and floats away from her body, she thinks about what it all could mean and remembers things she has read about such experiences.

The moment I thought about hesitation, my soaring stopped. I stopped my flight, consciously, in space. I didn't want to go any higher. As it was I could see the curvature of the Earth, and darkness on the other side of the globe. . . . I directed myself downward, back to my body. Slowly I descended. Slowly . . . down, down . . . gently through the space I wafted back to earth. The vibrations subsided . . . the rolling sensation of the undulating thought waves disappeared above me and with a soft fusion of contact that felt like a puff, I melded back into my body. . . . The silver cord melded into the flickering candlelight and I shook myself free of the concentration and looked over at David who was smiling.[11]

MacLaine and her friend David interpreted this as an experience showing that everything is energy, the body is just a temporary residence of the soul, this soul can be separated from the body and can be reincarnated into other bodies. It is seen as an indication that each person is, after all, really divine.[12] Death is not separation from God but just a transition from one experience to another in a long line of reincarnations till one finally finds total rest in realizing one's inherent divinity.[13]

Between her experience and the interpretative "authority" of "David," MacLaine has come to believe a great deal—much of it, as one can tell from her direct comments, uncongenial with, and even contradictory to, the beliefs of Blaise Pascal (the traditional beliefs of Christianity).

Both Pascal and MacLaine have had intense, ecstatic experiences. But what one has learned contradicts what the other has learned. One or both of them must be in error.

Pascal sees God as personal, triune, awesome in his power and his holiness; sin is very much an issue, as is God's forgiveness. MacLaine eventually concludes that she herself is God (and so is every person); sin is not an issue. Pascal believes in a God who creates; MacLaine believes in the power of each person to create her or his own reality. Pascal encounters God personally; MacLaine, in other trance experiences, encounters her Higher Self (the combination of all her incarnations, past and future) and learns directly from It (MacLaine does not use the personal pronoun for H.S., as she sometimes calls the tall, semiandrogynous figure she sees in trance states). Pascal says the Gospels are the only way to encounter and be kept by God. MacLaine consults not only her own Higher Self but also several channelers or mediums who allegedly channel wisdom from spiritual or extraterrestrial beings.

We simply cannot have it both ways. We cannot accept William James's position and say that both Pascal and MacLaine are justified in what they believe.

The Religious Authority of Religious Experience

The religious authority of religious experience is not absolute, neither for the person who has the experience nor for those who hear of these experiences. But such experiences do have evidential value, and they do need to be explained.[14] Something is going on. What is it? I will make some preliminary comments here, but we will have to wait till chapters six and fifteen to see this answer fleshed out.

Profound religious experiences like those of Pascal and MacLaine point to a capacity the human mind has for seemingly accessing a spiritual reality. Is this just an illusion? Is the mind tricking those who have these experiences? Are we just contemplating the machinations of our own brain pan? If there is a reality to which these experiences point, which reality is it—a pantheistic reality, a theistic reality or something else as yet unidentified or undefined? Is it possible that "lying spirits" are deluding our minds, keeping us from the truth? Is there a spiritual battle being waged over our soul, with good spirits wooing us one way and bad spirits another?

How does the evidence of these trance states square with other evidence that we have for how human beings behave? If we already have a very good idea of what the spiritual realm is like, how does our experience fit with what we believe or know from other sources? Is there any person—psychologist, priest, saint, religious expert—present or past, whom we believe enough to trust what he or she says about these matters?

As we will soon see, the fittingness of all the data and reasoned arguments that confront us should, I believe, carry the most weight. We cannot rely on any one type of "reason" for belief but must weigh all the "reasons" (with all the reasons *against* these reasons taken into account). Why should anyone believe anything at all?—when the "anything" is a foundational notion—is not a question to be answered lightly. Too much is at stake.

Whether we like it or not, we base our lives on beliefs.
We are presented with many alternatives, and our beliefs must
play an important part in which paths we choose. But beyond
a "passive belief," beyond an acceptance of whatever beliefs our
society, our environment, our friends might program into us,
we must *actively* seek Truth and find good reason for our
belief. For the beliefs programmed into us are likely
to be incomplete and misleading.

WILLIAMS STUDENT, 1991

———

The
Philosophic
Dimension

6

As a boy growing up on a Nebraska ranch, I learned about the outer world through the radio and a weekly Omaha newspaper. World War II played itself out for me through the newscasts from WMAX and WOW. But what I waited eagerly for were the radio dramas: *Jack Armstrong, the All American Boy, Sky King, Gangbusters* and *Mr. District Attorney*.

One winter a blizzard left deep drifts across the country roads. In the morning my pony could get me only within a mile of my school before belly-deep snow prevented further progress. There was nothing for me to do but return home. But how was I to face my mother? By the time I had traveled the two miles back to the ranch, I had the preface to my explanation—the opening words to *Mr. District Attorney:* "I swear to tell the truth, the whole truth and nothing but the truth."

The words were quite unnecessary. Mother had found out about the deep drifts that had piled up on the plains beyond the valley in which we lived. Before I could get the words out, she grabbed and hugged me and apologized for sending me out. A moment to savor in any child's life!

The Truth, the Whole Truth and Nothing But the Truth

We come finally to the nub of the issue. There are many causes operating in the development of our beliefs. Family, friends, the media, society, culture all impinge on us, and it is only within their context that our beliefs develop. The older we become, the more our mind and character mature, the more conscious we become of our beliefs and the more responsible we become for them.

Our hopes and desires—physical, aesthetic, intellectual, emotional—tug at us, demanding fulfillment. We want security, a sense of direction and purpose, a reason to go on living. We would like to be happy. Our beliefs are shaped by these wants and needs. Some of our beliefs may help us in the short run, but what about the long-run future? Will our beliefs sustain us after death, if indeed there is any conscious afterlife for us?

Our experience, the stuff of ordinary conscious life, weighs our beliefs, sometimes confirming them, sometimes challenging them, sometimes totally undermining the foundations on which our hopes have rested. Our religious experiences overwhelm us with their intensity without guaranteeing that what is intense points to the way things really are.

We can feel too frightened. We can become terrified by a sense of impending doom brought on by shadows cast by the rays of a streetlamp playing through the leaves outside our window. There is nothing there to fear. Our terror is ungrounded.

We can also feel too secure. Feeling a "holy" spirit fill the room, we are driven to our knees in adoration or we lift our hands in praise. All well and good. But like Pollyanna, we sometimes deceive ourselves, even shaping what we take to be our "religious" experience by naive hopes that refuse to be shattered on the anvil of reality.

Behind all these reasons, what we really need is the truth. Is there any hope of finding it?

X is true. In the process of analysis during my lecture/discussion, students come finally—if not sooner—to realize that truth is the real issue. If our parents have raised us to believe things that are untrue, they are not to be believed, not even if these beliefs have been reinforced by our friends, society and culture. If our hope is grounded in illusion, we ought to become disillusioned and find out what is really true. If we have misinterpreted our experience, we should search for the proper interpretation.

Few will disagree with this, but many still find the prospect problematic. Two different professors had opposite reactions to this prospect. After an analysis of reasons for beliefs, a professor of philosophy remarked, "You have spent forty-five minutes proving a tautology. Of course one ought to believe what is true. The question is, How do you know what is true?"[1] Another professor from the religion department asked rather snidely, "What do you mean by *truth?*"

I defined truth for the religion professor as propositional: a statement is true if what it says is so is so, or if what it says is not so is not so.[2] If I say it's raining outside and it is, the statement is true. I remarked that this was the basic understanding that undergirded most philosophy up through the end of the nineteenth century.[3] The professor charged this definition with naiveté. "There are lots of definitions of truth," he said. "Yours is only one. Truth is relative to the culture and the speaker. It's arrogant to think that one can squeeze truth into such a narrow compass."[4]

There is, of course, some validity to this charge. The nature of "truth" has been problematic for a long time.[5] But I insisted then, and I insist now, that the kind of "truth" that is required for belief is precisely this kind. The philosophy professor is much closer to understanding what my analysis of reasons amounts to. It is axiomatic (perhaps even a tautology) to say that one ought to believe the truth.[6] The problem is that in today's world, especially on today's campuses, the concept of belief is separated from the concept of truth.

"It's true for you; it's not true for me" is a common response from students confronted by the claims of any exclusive religion. "Sure, the

Muslims believe all sorts of odd things," students say. "At least I think they do. But look, it's their right to do so. It's fine for them. It's not my thing, but why should it be?"

Students have to be convinced that truth is even relevant to belief. An analysis such as the one I have presented in chapters two through five is one way to help students see that they themselves evaluate their own reasons for beliefs from the standpoint of truth. So the real question is not "Why should Islam be my thing?" but "Why shouldn't it be?" What if it's true that Islam is the true religion? What if "there is no God but Allah, and Muhammad is his prophet"? This claim cannot be dismissed with "It's true for you but not for me." If it's true, it's true. And here's the rub: it will cost you dearly if you don't accept it. If Islam is true, Allah demands and deserves worship and obedience from everyone. The truth-claim is universal, absolute and objective.

The same is the case with every religion, even those like Hinduism or Buddhism that do not emphasize the "truth"-claims of their grasp of reality.[7] If, for example, a fulfilled life can be realized with yogic meditation, if this will improve your lot in subsequent incarnations, if in your essence you are really god, what a waste not to believe and act on that! You will have to keep being reincarnated in a lower form until you "get it right."

To point the question boldly, take the issue of God's existence: "In the case of contradictories, no middle ground is possible. The theistic affirmation *God exists* and the atheistic denial *God does not exist* stand in contradiction to one another: both cannot be true and both cannot be false; if one is true; the other must be false."[8]

The same is true of the fate of human beings at death. One is either resurrected or not, reincarnated or not, rendered personally extinct at death or not.[9] Moreover, if one of them is true, the others must be false. They all may be false and some other fate await us, like "living" a shadowy existence in a parallel universe; but they can't all be true. The question becomes especially pointed when the issue is, If there is an afterlife, how should one believe and behave now so as to spend that afterlife in bliss rather than agony?

All of this seems fairly clear. We should believe the truth. But that resolved, there remain two questions: (1) What is the truth we should believe? (2) How can I recognize it? The first question will be treated in part two of this book. Here we turn to the second. To put it in the words of Mortimer Adler: "By what means or criteria can we determine whether this or that proposition is true or false?"[10] Among the criteria, the following should be foundational.

X is reasonable. What people believe is reasonable varies somewhat from person to person. After seeing someone fall from a seventh-story window, most people would say it's reasonable to believe that the person is either dead or severely injured. That would conform to what one believes about height, falls, the structure of the human body and the nature of the ground being struck. Throughout our life we come to thousands of reasonable conclusions, most of which prove to be true. Our car falters to a stop on a highway; we look at the gas gauge and say, "Oh, no. I'm out of gas!" The electricity suddenly goes off when we turn on the air conditioner; we say, "The circuit was overloaded and a fuse is blown [a circuit breaker has tripped]." All of our grades on papers and tests have been Bs; we conclude that we will receive a B in the course. All are reasonable conclusions.

Reasonable but not necessarily true. The person who fell may have been caught in a firefighters' net. The gas gauge in the car may have malfunctioned and a faulty fuel pump may be the problem. The electricity may have been cut off because lightning struck a transformer two miles down the line. The professor may decide to grade "on the curve" and actually give you an A. Time and further investigation will reveal what the truth is. But short of overwhelming evidence, we still make reasonable conclusions based on the data we have.

There is an important carryover from the function of our reason in daily living to its function in more complex religious matters. We take what seems to us to be the character of the world, of God and of human beings, and we evaluate religious claims on that basis.

There is nothing odd or inappropriate about believing propositions that seem "reasonable" to us and doubting those that don't. If, for example, I have experienced human beings as both loving and hating, and someone tells me that human beings are really all good at heart, my doubt mechanism is immediately triggered. Whoever makes such a claim about human beings will have to do some very fancy dancing to show me how my former belief that human beings are a complex mixture of good and bad is mistaken.

Reason in this broad sense, then, performs a task of checking what I think I already know with what I am being offered as a development of that belief or an alternative to it. In the active and proper use of reason, everything that one believes acts as a check on anything further or contrary that one is asked to believe. In the process of reasoning, we often change our mind. New data, recognition of a particular failure of reason to function properly, a larger context in which to place what we know—these all serve to modify our beliefs. And they should. We are never in possession of the whole of reality; we need to expand our understanding and correct it where necessary.

Sometimes in religious matters we are asked to believe things that at first seem unreasonable. The proposition "Jesus died and was resurrected a few days later," for example, will not look reasonable to a naturalist (a person who believes that nature does not behave like that and that nature is, after all, all that is). In fact, the resurrection did not look reasonable to Jesus' chief disciples when some women came and told them that that was what had happened to Jesus. Later these disciples changed their mind. Their own context was enlarged when Jesus later actually appeared to them. Or so the story goes. (I will look again at this issue in chapter eleven to see if there is any "reason" to think the resurrection actually happened.) If it did happen, then certain things follow: it tends to validate Jesus' teachings and his self-understanding. If it did not happen, then certain other things follow: for example, the belief of the early church that he did rise from the dead must somehow be explained. (Such an explanation is more difficult to come up with than many imagine.) Moreover, if it did not happen, then those who believe he did rise are "to be pitied more than all men" (1 Corinthians 15:19).

Human reason in the broad sense has many limitations. For one thing, we often make mistakes; we don't notice how something we believe about one matter should affect something we believe about another. Second, it is limited by the information it has at hand. No one is likely to believe the tenets of Buddhism if they have never been exposed to any aspect of the religion.[11] No one will see the "truth" of the Christian faith unless they put themselves in the way of finding out about its claims. Third, human reason cannot generate the content of any religious truth. It may apprehend truth through experience or revelation, but it is not a source. Reason may also provide the intellectual models (for example, the doctrine of the Trinity) used to understand scriptural statements in a consistent way. But if the human mind is a source of anything, it is not because of reason but because of imagination. And imagination may be rich in suggestivity, but the reality of any product of human imagination—as glorious as those products often are when developed as stories and hypotheses of science—is subject to all the tests of truth we are examining in this chapter.

Unless one is convinced that the *source* of a matter offered for belief is itself a guarantee of its truth, the *source* of truth is not in and of itself relevant to determining its truth. It makes no difference whether the idea came from an alleged scripture, a newspaper, a child, a philosopher, an otherwise untrustworthy person. If the idea is true, it's true. In fact, all the checks for truth should be used on the source itself. Is the source self-consistent? Does it give a coherent picture of what it proposes? Does what it says about any given matter correspond with what you believe from other sources to be accurate? Is there any reason to think the new source is correct and your old idea incorrect?

Reason in the broad sense, then, is a criterion for evaluating truth-claims, but not a source of these claims.

X is logical. There is a narrow sense of reason that is more fundamental than the broad sense we looked at above. Reason is bounded by the laws of logic. These laws can be stated briefly and simply. They are easy to understand, because they are the very principles of our understanding.

1. *X* is *X.* (the law of identity)
2. *X* is not both *X* and not-*X.* (the law of noncontradiction)
3. Every declarative sentence is either true or false. (the law of the excluded middle)

The basic notion is that something cannot both be and not be at the same time. This can be endlessly illustrated. For example:

1. A lead pencil is a lead pencil.
2. A lead pencil is not both a lead pencil and not a lead pencil [a computer, a crayon or some other object].
3. This object in my hand either is a lead pencil or isn't.

In brief, however, it is the principle of noncontradiction that is the chief test of truth. If someone proclaims, for example, that both resurrection and reincarnation are true, then he or she will have to show how both of them could be so without violating the principle of noncontradiction. Various attempts might be made. One could say that the term *resurrection* and the term *reincarnation* really mean the same thing. This is refuted when one examines the meaning of each term. One could say that resurrection and reincarnation perform the same function in Christianity and New Age thinking: they give hope to people in this life. This would be true; but now we are talking about the *function* of a belief (or the truth about how a belief functions) and not about the *truth* of the belief. Oddly, reincarnation in Hinduism does not function to give hope but to confirm the Hindu notion that it takes a long time for a human soul to realize the perfection of its essential deity. In any case, where *resurrection* is understood in a Christian sense and *reincarnation* in a Hindu or New Age sense, the two possibilities for human afterlife cannot both be true.

A third attempt to reconcile resurrection and reincarnation would be to say a soul is reincarnated until it finally reaches perfection and then is resurrected. But while this may be held by some theosophists, if it were true, then what both resurrection and reincarnation entail as understood by traditional Christians and Hindus (resurrection first entails the permanence of the individual person; reincarnation entails the impermanence of the individual person) would not be true.

Logic, then, serves as a rational check on one's belief. If certain elements of a person's belief, when elaborated, are seen to be contradictory, then one or more of those elements are untrue. Logic does not tell which of any two or three are false; it just locates the problem. Its function is, nonetheless, vital. One violates logic only at great peril of being profoundly deluded.

There is empirical evidence for X. The foundational notions of religions are often not susceptible to empirical test. What evidence—detectable by the five senses—can be given for the existence of a God who is pure spirit or for the notion that fundamental reality is really not material but "ideal" or spiritual? Still, some important religious beliefs do have aspects that, at least in principle, empirical evidence would tend to confirm or disconfirm. This is especially true of the "religions of the book"—Judaism, Christianity and Islam.

These religions make claims about events in space-time history—for example, the exodus of a large body of people from Egypt to Palestine; the flight of Jesus and his parents from Israel to Egypt; the existence of a "Jesus of Nazareth" who taught, performed marvelous works, was crucified, was buried and rose from the dead; the existence of a "Muhammad" in the Middle East. There is more evidence external to the scriptures bearing testimony to these last two than to the first two. In "historical religions"—that is, religions that claim religious significance for historical events—a substantiation of the event itself is relevant.

If Jesus rose from the dead, for example, it means something. Exactly what is not obvious from the event itself. But for such an event to have the significance attributed to it by Christianity, it must have happened. If evidence could show that it didn't happen (if, for example, someone were to produce the bones of Jesus), then much of the New Testament's teaching about how God has forgiven sins is simply falsified. Granted, at this stage in history the task of providing evidence that any given set of bones are the bones of Jesus would be formidable beyond measure. Still, the principle holds: the essence of the Christian faith rises or falls on the historicity of this event.

Occasionally what we have learned through scientific analysis may conflict with what is claimed by religions. If, for example, it could be demonstrated that human evolution has actually occurred with natural selection operating as a "blind watchmaker," along the lines described by Richard Dawkins, then the belief in a God who designed and created the universe and human beings is, if not disproved, at least undermined.[12] We would in fact become subject to what James Rachels takes as inevitable: "After Darwin, we can no longer think of ourselves as occupying a special place in creation—instead, we must realize that we are products of the same evolutionary forces, working blindly and without purpose, that shaped the rest of the animal kingdom."[13] And we would have to put up with whatever significance this "fact" has for our own purposes and moral motions. But the whole enterprise of evolutionary theory has itself come under fire as inadequately grounded in data and flawed in reason.[14]

If we could observe major structural changes occurring in the present biosphere, that would be data for evolution. We can't, or at least haven't yet. If we had a fossil record that contained one or more clear sequences of gradual change from one species to another, that would be data for evolution. We don't. In other words, theoretically there ought to be certain kinds of empirical data supporting evolution. If they are there, we haven't found them yet. The point is this: certain kinds of empirical data, if they existed, would severely challenge the justification for certain kinds of religious belief.

A third way in which empirical evidence relates to the justification of belief is "personal" experience, especially when that experience seems religious in nature. That brings us to the next philosophic reason.

I have experienced X. As we have seen in our discussion of experience in chapters four and five, experience plays a major role in molding our beliefs. Those who have had a profound "religious" experience not only testify to the "experience" itself but come away with a sense of "what" they have experienced. Some conclude that death is just a transition to another realm; others that they have seen and talked with Jesus or the Virgin Mary or their Higher Self or a spirit guide.

The question is, Can these experiences be trusted to give accurate insight into the nature of reality? Unfortunately, the answer is a very guarded yes and no. Let's take the yes first.

Yes, these experiences testify clearly to human beings' ability to have exalted states of awareness. There are forms of consciousness that go beyond simple waking consciousness, dreaming consciousness and unconsciousness. Whatever else we might conclude about these experiences, they have occurred. If we as human beings have this capacity, then at least we can conclude it is possible that what we experience really does provide a glimpse of a deeper level of reality than is accessible by normal waking and dreaming.

Second, the lives of those having the experiences are transformed. Pascal, for example, turned his attention solely to higher pursuits after his experience. No more gaming with the royalty for him. In fact, he turned his life over totally to the clarification and defense of the Christian faith—not that he abandoned his interest in science, by the way, as is sometimes charged by modern naturalists bemoaning the loss of the scientific efforts of a brilliant mind. MacLaine, while not abandoning her career as a performer, has become a prolific writer promoting New Age ideas and practices.

The problem is that, though religious experience may give some evidence for the existence of a transcendent realm, perhaps even the existence of God, the experience itself does not guarantee its truthfulness. Pascal and MacLaine have come away with radically different, quite contradictory, views of reality. They can't both be true.

Still, if Christianity is true, then an experience such as that of Pascal is entirely possible. Moreover, the Christian understanding of reality has a way of explaining why MacLaine's experience is possible without necessarily leading to the conclusions she draws. Christians believe that there are fallen spiritual beings (demons) that can and do deceive people. It is quite possible that such deception is what has happened in MacLaine's case, they might well say. Moreover, the human mind can play tricks. We can deceive ourselves by our own desire for something to be the case that isn't the case. MacLaine's visions may have been triggered by her own overweening curiosity about the spirit world and her own vivid imagination. By her own admission, she has usually been accompanied by a New Age believer when her trance experiences have occurred. Perhaps the specific experiences were triggered by hypnosis and suggestions from her friends and spiritual advisers. Finally, though I take MacLaine to be telling the truth about the experiences she has had, some who claim to have special religious experiences may simply be committing fraud on the gullible, often for monetary gain.

On the other hand, from a New Age perspective MacLaine's experiences are entirely possible. So are Pascal's. Here, however, Pascal's experiences are not so likely to be attributed to "lying spirits." Rather, a typical New Age response would be to accept them as "true for the person having the experience." Pascal's spirit guide is "Jesus Christ" or "the God of Abraham, Isaac and Jacob." Each person gets his or her own vision of reality; and each vision is equally valid, equally true for the person having it. Of course, the content of Pascal's experience contradicts the content of typical New Age experience, but for those New Agers like MacLaine this poses no problem. For them there is no universal truth about reality. Reality is what each person makes it to be.

We have already seen how unlikely this is. Science would not work in a world where reincarnation and resurrection (and extinction, too) were all true. The universe would not be sufficiently uniform.

The point is that if a belief about reality is true, then some specific types of experience are fully coherent with that belief. In fact, these experiences should be expected. If they do not occur, then the belief is likely to be false. If Christians did *not* experience a sense of relief when they grasped the notion that their sins are forgiven—not just ignored or worked off by good deeds—then it would be odd indeed.

If no one were ever deluded by false belief triggered by misinterpreted experience, it would also be odd.

Intense personal and religious experience, then, must be incorporated into the larger pattern of justification of belief. Even though these intense experiences carry the power to convince the one having the experience, they must be themselves subject to postexperience reflection. If there are good reasons to suspect that the experience is misleading (as there are, for example, of those who say they have been contacted by extraterrestrial beings that emerge from flying saucers), then the experience, no matter how intense, should not be trusted. A simple "epistemology of ecstasy" is an inadequate justification for serious religious beliefs.

Best Explanation: The Final Frontier

X gives the best explanation for the tough issues of life. This is the capstone reason justifying any given belief or set of beliefs. Rather than standing alone, however, it attempts to put all the other "good" reasons together in one all encompassing "best" reason.

Beliefs arise in various ways—from our social environment, our reflection on experience, the ideas we garner from the media (books, magazines, newspapers, television, movies). But the key that ties together all the information and pressure toward and against belief is the sense we get that any given belief provides the "best explanation" of what needs explaining. The best explanation for a simple matter such as why our car has stalled accounts for all the data we have, even at times suggesting ways we might further check the correctness of our belief. The "best explanation" for an ultimately serious matter such as what happens after death does the same thing.

The characteristics of that "best explanation" include the following:
☐ accounts for all the data we hold to be relevant—historical, scientific, personally "experiential"
☐ is internally consistent
☐ is consistent with all the other matters that we hold to be true
☐ provides along with our other beliefs a more coherent picture of

the world, ourselves and others than any alternative[15]

Two things should be obvious about these criteria. First, they are intended to be exhaustive. That is, a "best explanation" has to meet a very high standard. Second, it may be difficult to discern just when this standard has been met. Some aspects of the "best explanation" standard will, of course, be easier to meet than others. Self-consistency, for example, is likely to be more readily come by than accounting for all the data or even having enough relevant data at hand. But when the notion of "best explanation" is applied to any given belief, there is at least a reasonable chance that progress can be made toward justifying one's belief or providing justification for changing one's mind.[16]

In part two I will try to show how the Christian faith does indeed provide the "best explanation" for several issues: the identity of Jesus, the historicity of the Gospels, the foundation for morality, the possibility of miracles and the actuality of at least one (the resurrection of Jesus), and the experience of Christian believers. Of course, the "best explanation" will, in the final analysis, have to be the best explanation for all our experience, all our questions, all of what we think needs explaining. But a book that tried to do that would never be finished. So part two does not claim to provide the best explanation of everything, only to show that for some of the most basic issues, Christianity does provide the best explanation. Because these issues are so fundamental, the best explanation for them lends considerable credence to the truth of the whole of the Christian faith.[17]

Why Should Anyone Believe Christianity?
Part II

The Gospels justify neither resignation nor scepticism.
Rather they bring before our eyes, in a very different fashion
from what is customary in chronicles and presentations of history,
the historical person of Jesus with the utmost vividness.
Quite clearly what the Gospels report concerning the message,
the deeds and history of Jesus is still distinguished by an
authenticity, a freshness, and a distinctiveness not in any way
effaced by the Church's Easter faith. These features point us
directly to the earthly figure of Jesus.

GÜNTHER BORNKAMM, *JESUS OF NAZARETH*

————

The
Gospels as
Reliable
History

7

T hroughout the previous six chapters I have taken a skeptical
attitude to belief, especially religious belief. Have I been too
skeptical? I don't think so.

Throughout the world today, the options for belief in the area of
religion are legion. Let's say you are a student at Whatever State
University. Your biology teacher is likely to be an atheist; your math
professor attends the local Lutheran church; your English teacher
makes snide remarks about anyone who still believes there is a God,
or even truth for that matter; your lab instructor in chemistry med-
itates on a Sanskrit mantra every morning; your history professor is
a devout Muslim; and your comparative religion teacher thinks that
all religions have symbolic, if not literal, truth. To stay sane, Sam, your
roommate, has totally abandoned any interest at all in religious subjects. And you, a serious believer in the faith in which you were raised,
have developed serious doubts.

If you are in this situation, are you justified in having doubts? Yes, if you have not at least begun to think clearly about what you do and do not believe about the tough questions: Is there a God? What is God (if there is one) like? How should I live my life if there is/is not a God? Do I have any obligations to anyone but myself—my parents, my employer, maybe even God?

Has your roommate really escaped his responsibility by ceasing to think about the big issues of life? No, he has just shown his lack of intellectual and moral stamina. Sam still believes—at this point at least implicitly—in the propriety of his flight from a thoughtful faith. Is he justified in being thoughtless? The question answers itself.

In a pluralistic society—and all of the world touched by modernity is to some extent pluralistic—justifying one's faith (regardless of what it is) can be difficult. It is at least an awesome task fraught with danger. If as Christianity teaches, for example, a holy God holds us responsible for our beliefs, then the weight of our responsibility is great indeed.[1] Neither you nor your roommate can get off the hook. Are there, then, good reasons for believing one thing rather than another?

In the previous chapter we saw that in the final analysis, the only reason for believing something is that it is true. Then we examined several kinds of tests for truth: logical consistency, coherence of our beliefs with each other to form a systematic whole, and the explanatory power of our beliefs. In short, any argument for our beliefs should (1) be based on the best evidence, (2) be validly argued and (3) refute the strongest objections that can be made. The belief most likely to be true is the belief that gives the "best explanation" of all that we would like explained, especially the tough issues that touch our lives most deeply.

We turn, then, in this section to examine the truth-claims of the Christian faith. Are there any good reasons for believing Christianity to be true?

Evaluating the Truth-Claims of Christian Faith

There are at least four basic reasons that Christians can be justified in believing the fundamental tenets and practicing the lifestyle of the Christian faith. We will examine each of them in the remaining chapters of this book:

1. Jesus himself: his character of wisdom and compassion, the method and content of his teaching, his resurrection.

2. The historical reliability of the Gospels.

3. The internal consistency and coherence of the Christian worldview and its power to provide the best explanation of the tough issues of life.

4. The testimony of individual Christians and of countless Christian communities that, down through the ages, exhibit the transforming power of God in and among his faithful believers.

Jesus the Reason

Put simply, the best reason for believing that the Christian religion is true is Jesus, and the best reason for believing in Jesus is Jesus himself.

That may sound strange. How can Jesus be a reason? In what kind of argument for the truth of a religion is it possible that the best reason could be a person?

That's not quite the right question. It is better to ask, In what kind of religion is a person the best reason for believing it? Arguments and the reasons that go with them depend on the character of the truth to be proved. Christianity, it turns out, is itself fundamentally about a person—the person of Jesus. Christianity proclaims that God has made himself known in many ways—through the Hebrews, through the events of history, through the shape and form of the universe itself, through visions and personal encounters with God. But he has most supremely made himself known in and through Jesus Christ.

Though it may seem strange at first, the argument of part two will attempt to demonstrate this: anyone who knows Jesus knows that Christianity is true.

But then, how does one come to know Jesus? That is the question this and the next three chapters will try to answer. I will begin by addressing what we might call the "facts of the case" and end by stressing that getting to know a person (living or dead) is more than getting to know facts. Getting to know a person is beginning more and more to penetrate the character of that person and realizing that the other person is beginning to penetrate your character as well. We only really know those who become open to us as we become open with them. But that is to get ahead of ourselves. Let's look at the facts.

The Reliability of the Sources

The only source of detailed information about Jesus is the Bible, in particular the New Testament. Within the New Testament are four Gospels, narratives of what Jesus did and said, a group of letters from the apostles (especially Paul), an account of the spread of the early church and a highly symbolic vision about the end times. Of these, the Gospels contain the vast bulk of what can be known about Jesus. Three of these Gospels, called the Synoptic Gospels (Matthew, Mark and Luke), are structured very much like each other, and their contents overlap so that we often can find several accounts of the same events. All of them, for example, devote the most space to the last week of Jesus' life.

As a source for knowledge about Jesus there is absolutely no substitute for the Gospels themselves. I invite any of my readers to put down this book and turn directly to them. They are not just filled with information about Jesus; they are spellbinding. Reader after reader will testify that the Gospels carry within themselves the power of conviction. To those who are thirsting after the truth about life and are willing to act on what they learn, the truth of Jesus Christ proclaimed by the Gospels comes as living water. I invite skeptics to drink deep of the Gospels before concluding that little about Jesus, little about the meaning of life, can be known.

For centuries the question "Who is Jesus?" was considered unproblematic. Jesus was precisely who the Bible and the church, following the Bible, said he was: the incarnate Son of God, Second Person of the Trinity, fully God and fully human. He lived an exemplary life, performed the signs and miracles that the Gospels said he did, taught what the New Testament said he taught, called together a group of disciples and was crucified, giving his life as a ransom for many. He was resurrected three days later, continued to teach his disciples and then ascended back to God. He will come again to wrap up history and to usher in the full reign of God over all reality.

Today, in fact since the Enlightenment, the question "Who is Jesus?" has been fraught with difficulty. Students now taking courses in religion in the university come away with the impression that the New Testament is simply not to be trusted as a record of what Jesus did or said. It is "full of contradictions," replete with stories of highly unlikely events such as alleged miracles, the repository of a mythical notion of God and his relation to history. Students who enter college believing the Bible are often shocked when they first hear these notions from their friends or from their professors. But whether students take these courses or not, the general impression among most students is that the Bible is not a book that they need to reckon with as a guide to life.

The historical reliability of the Gospels is crucial. Other ancient sources such as Pliny, Tacitus and Josephus confirm the fact of Jesus' existence in the time and place Christians have always believed. But the Gospels are our only source of detailed information about what Jesus did and said. If we cannot trust the picture the Gospels draw, we cannot know who Jesus was, and thus Jesus cannot be a reason for belief.

The issue is not easy to tackle. Scholars of every persuasions have produced a wealth of research. A veritable mountain of books have come from a wide variety of perspectives.[2] Some are convinced that the traditional picture is true, others reconstruct Jesus in the light of their own methodology, and still others argue that little at all can be known about Jesus. In recent years we have been given a host of portraits of Jesus: Jesus the revolutionary (S. G. S. Brandon, *Jesus and the Zealots*), Jesus the Jewish holy man (Geza Vermes, *Jesus the Jew*), Jesus the wandering Cynic preacher (Burton Mack, *A Myth of Inno-*

cence), Jesus the Jewish Cynic and peasant teacher (John Dominic Crossan, *The Historical Jesus*), Jesus the Essene (Barbara Thiering, *Jesus the Man*), Jesus the simple Galilean holy man (A. N. Wilson, *Jesus*), Jesus the Cosmic and New Age Christ (David Spangler, *Reflections on the Christ*) and many more.[3] I can only scratch the surface with what follows here. Readers who want to pursue the subject further may wish to start with some of the books listed in the bibliography.[4]

For two centuries skeptics have given a number of reasons for suspecting that the Gospels are not to be taken at face value. Six of them continue to undergird modern skepticism:

1. We do not have the original manuscripts of the New Testament; in the process of copying, many errors were introduced.

2. Translators have introduced errors into the Bible. Besides, there are so many translations, how does one know which one to rely on?

3. The Gospels present a Jesus who performed miracles. We now know that miracles cannot happen. The stories must have been made up by the Gospel writers or their sources. If we cannot trust the stories of miracles, we can trust neither the narratives of other events in Jesus' life nor the teachings of their main protagonist.

4. The Gospels are full of contradictions.

5. The Gospels were not written until many years after the events they record. We cannot trust the accuracy of the writers' or translators' memory.

6. The Gospels tell the story of Jesus from the perspective of the leaders of the early church, who were writing to buttress their own authority.

I will deal with the first four of these six reasons one by one. The second two I will deal with together. They are part of a larger issue and can best be considered if we look at the specific picture of Jesus that the Gospels draw.

Text and Translation
The first reason for skepticism—the New Testament text is unreliable—is not generally accepted by even the most critical of modern

scholars. Though many people today will give it as a reason for rejecting the Christian faith, they are usually doing so out of ignorance. In most scholarly works of the past few decades it does not appear as a reason for rejecting the historicity of the Gospels. The fact is that there are some five thousand manuscripts (deriving from a variety of much earlier sources) that contain texts of the New Testament documents, many more than exist for any other ancient literary work.[5] After decades of intense study of these manuscripts, most scholars have concluded that the text of the New Testament is probably the most accurate ancient document we have.[6] In short, most New Testament scholars have concluded that we know essentially what the original writers wrote.

The second reason for skepticism—that the translations are unreliable—is easily put aside. In fact, even on the face of it the reason given for skepticism is actually a reason for confidence. The very fact that the Bible has been translated so often—but so uniformly in meaning—is an excellent reason to conclude that translators today are doing an excellent job. Just compare any English translation of the Gospel of Mark, say, with any other and it will immediately be evident that they are translating the same Greek text and that the meanings coming through are almost, if not exactly, identical. There are a handful of problematic passages on which the translation is contested, but no major event or teaching is at stake. There is every reason to believe that even in English we can know what the New Testament writers wrote. Of course, we need to understand what the text *means*. Interpretation is always an issue. But there is no reason to reject the reliability of the New Testament on the basis of the fact that we do not read Greek.

The Impossibility of Miracle
The third reason for skepticism is very different in character from the first two. It presumes a world in which miracles—events that do not conform to the way the universe regularly operates—cannot occur. That is, when the Bible records Jesus' healings or his casting out of

demons, the account cannot be taken at face value. Perhaps something very natural happened that looked *unnatural* or *supernatural;* perhaps the Gospel writers fabricated the stories to inspire awe or to encourage belief in a new religious sect; perhaps the stories were intended, like parables or fiction or poetry, only to carry a moral, not to narrate an actual event. Whatever is the case, if something can't happen, it didn't.

And if something didn't happen, it cannot be a reason for believing anything. Interestingly, the apostle Paul makes this very point with regard to the most astounding miracle story of all, the resurrection:

> If there is no resurrection of the dead, then not even Christ has been raised. And if Christ has not been raised, our preaching is useless and so is your faith. More than that, we are then found to be false witnesses about God, for we have testified about God that he raised Christ from the dead. (1 Corinthians 15:13-15)

Just in case we didn't get that the first time, through, Paul immediately repeats his argument:

> But he did not raise him if in fact the dead are not raised. For if the dead are not raised, then Christ has not been raised either. And if Christ has not been raised, your faith is futile; you are still in your sins. Then those who have fallen asleep in Christ [that is, have died as believers] are lost. If only for this life we have hope in Christ, we are to be pitied more than all men. (1 Corinthians 15:15-19)

For Paul, the resurrection of Jesus Christ is a vital event. If it happened, it means that human sins have been paid for; Christ's death was sufficient; people can be redeemed. If he was not raised from the dead, then his life and death were no more significant than the life and death of any other good person. The whole fabric of the Christian faith is not just torn but shredded. It should be abandoned. For Paul, therefore, it is vital that miracles be possible.

But are they? Can miracles—events that do not conform to the regular way the universe operates—happen? How is one to know?

Actually, there is no way we as human beings can *know* with absolute certainty that miracles cannot happen. We would have to know everything about the way the universe, reality itself, works. No one has that kind of knowledge. No reputable physicist—not even Stephen Hawking—will say he possesses this kind of knowledge of the physical nature of the universe. Even if one could find the final formula that would unite our knowledge of all the forces and all the matter we can detect, we could not be certain that there is not behind it all an undetectable force or mind or god who brought it all into being and can intervene in its processes.

The idea that miracles cannot happen is an article of faith. It goes beyond our knowledge. That does not mean that it is not true. Rather, it is either true or false that miracles cannot happen. In fact, even if no miracle had ever occurred at any time or place so far in the universe and we actually knew this to be true (which we don't and can't, but let's waive that), it would still be possible that miracles *could* occur.

What saves Christians as well as others from utter skepticism with regard to miracles, however, is not the principle that miracles *can* occur but rather the evidence that miracles *have* occurred.

For the greatest miracle of all, Paul willingly cites evidence:

For what I received I passed on to you as of first importance: that Christ died for our sins according to the Scriptures, that he was buried, that he was raised on the third day according to the Scriptures, and that he appeared to Peter, and then to the Twelve. After that, he appeared to more than five hundred of the brothers at the same time, most of whom are still living, though some have fallen asleep. Then he appeared to James, then to all the apostles, and last of all he appeared to me also, as to one abnormally born. (1 Corinthians 15:3-7)

The case against miracles must deal with the evidence for miracles. It cannot proceed on the basis of the general principle that miracles can't happen, for that general principle is itself subject to disproof. The first actual miracle disproves the principle. So the issue is, Have there been any miracles? More specifically, did Jesus really die and then rise from the dead?

I will deal with this issue later in the book. For now it is enough to note that the historicity of the record of the Gospels ought not be rejected on the basis of the prior principle that miracles cannot occur.

Contradictions

The fourth reason for skepticism, that the Gospels are full of contradictions, is simply not true as stated. It is, unfortunately, a very common misconception. I suspect this is the reason that university students who are not believers most frequently give when they are challenged to read the Bible or to heed one of its teachings. When I hear this given as an objection to reading the Bible, I usually say, "Oh, that's interesting. What contradictions did you have in mind?" Often no response is given. When one does come, it usually turns out to be something that is either not a contradiction at all—even on the face of it—or not a contradiction when the context and intent of the passages are considered.[7]

Some alleged contradictions in the Gospels are like the old conundrum "Where did Cain get his wife?" They are not contradictions, just issues the Bible does not address. There are lots of these questions. What did Jesus do during the years between age twelve and the beginning of his ministry some twenty years later? Why didn't Jesus heal all the sick in Israel? Or when did Jesus come to recognize that he had a special relationship to God?

Other proposed examples concern details that are inconsequential; they are based on an idea of accuracy that is misguided. For example, did the four men who lowered the paralytic through the roof of the house "dig through the roof" (reflecting a Galilean roof type) or take off "the tile" (reflecting a more Mediterranean type)? Mark (2:4), possibly writing for Palestinian readers, says the former; Luke (5:19), writing for a more generic Greek and Roman audience, says the latter. Both are trying to explain the extraordinary effort the men decided to make to get help from Jesus for their friend. Did they "dig through" or take off "the tile"? Or did they do both? The point of the event remains intact despite the difference in detail.[8]

Still, after all the simple confusions of modern readers have been addressed, some difficulties remain. Each one, however, must be addressed separately. Some easily yield under analysis. Others are more problematic. But none of them—nor all of them put together—is severe enough to cast doubt on the basic historical reliability of the Gospels.

Take one that has puzzled me. Luke says Quirinius was governor of Syria when Joseph and Mary went to Bethlehem to be taxed. Other sources from the time indicate that Quirinius was governor from A.D. 6 to 9. This, of course, would be several years after Jesus' birth. One scholar who has investigated this contradiction (not, note, of the Bible with itself but of the Bible with external, historical sources) has noted that Quirinius had been "leading military expeditions in the eastern provinces of the Roman empire a decade earlier" and that perhaps he was some type of "governor" before he was appointed to a "more formal" term. Of course, it is just as possible that the extrabiblical sources are in error as that Luke got it wrong.[9]

Another alleged contradiction that has puzzled readers is the different instructions that Jesus gave his disciples before he sent them on a mission. Did he tell them to take one staff and sandals (Mark) or no staff and no sandals (Matthew) or no staff, with no mention of sandals at all (Luke)? Because this appears to be a violation of the law of noncontradiction (see chapter six), the allegation appears significant. Here is how Craig Blomberg addresses the issue:

> The urgency of their mission [as described in Matthew 11] is to be visibly highlighted by their travelling unencumbered by unnecessary clothing or baggage; not even "sandals" or "a staff" for walking is permitted (verse 10). Luke agrees with the prohibition of the staff, omits all reference to footwear and otherwise greatly curtails his parallel (Lk. 9:1-6). Mark's account is slightly longer than Luke's but not nearly as elaborate as Matthew's (Mk. 6:6b-13). Yet in Mark, Jesus does permit both staff and sandals (verses 8-9). Surely, if ever there were an unassailable contradiction in the gospels, this would be it.

Nevertheless, it is hard to imagine Matthew or Luke editing Mark and rescinding Jesus' permission to take at least shoes and walking stick; a change from a more severe restriction to a lesser one would be the natural development. Moreover, Luke 10:1-24 describes a very similar commission—this time of seventy-two disciples—which Matthew's account of the charge to the twelve (9:37—10:16) often echoes. These echoes sometimes create greater parallelism between Matthew's sermon to the twelve and Luke's commission to the seventy-two than between Matthew's sermon to the twelve and Luke's version of the same sermon. The most obvious illustration of this parallelism is the famous saying about the plentiful harvest with few labourers (Mt. 9:37-38; Lk. 10:2; no parallel in Mk. 6 or Lk. 9). Since the seventy-two most likely included the twelve (cf. Lk. 10:17 and 23), an attractive hypothesis suggests that Matthew has combined some of Jesus' instructions to the twelve with some of those to the seventy-two. On the one occasion staff and shoes were permitted; on the other they were forbidden. Since all Matthew implies is that these are commands given by Jesus to the twelve in preparation for mission, one can hardly accuse him of error, even if he does not spell out the two stages of mission in the same way that Luke does. Previous examples of this kind of "telescoping" in Matthew have already appeared (see above, pp. 134-138 [in Blomberg]), so a further illustration should cause little surprise. Luke has then apparently edited his ninth chapter much as he did his trial narrative; assimilating some of the wording from the second commissioning speech into the first. Such practices scarcely discredited the historical reputation of ancient writers in the eyes of their contemporaries (cf. above, p. 135), so it is unfair to malign them today by applying anachronistic standards of historiography.[10]

The problem seems less difficult to me than it does to Blomberg. In all three accounts of Jesus' instructions—one staff or two, sandals or no sandals—the urgency of the mission and the necessity of relying on God's provision are what is at stake. The Gospel writers agree on that; the details seem to me to be inconsequential.

Perhaps the most troubling internal difficulty faced by those who accept the Bible's historical reliability is the reconciliation of the accounts of the resurrection. It and the crucifixion preceding it are the best attested single events in the Gospels. The story is told four times, each time with a host of similar details but also each time from a slightly different perspective and with a few unique details, some of which do not set easily with other details. At the tomb itself, was there one "young man dressed in a white robe" (Mark 16:5), one angel whose "clothes were white as snow" (Matthew 28:3), "two men in clothes that gleamed like lightning" (Luke 24:4) or "two angels in white" (John 20:12)? Did Jesus make his resurrection appearances only in Galilee (Matthew 28:16; Mark 16:7),[11] only in the area of Jerusalem (Luke 24) or in both (John 20—21)? Did the women tell (Matthew 28:10, 16; Luke 24:9; John 20:2) or not tell (Mark 16:8) what they saw at the tomb?

Answers to these questions are not easy.[12] Still, there is a basic unity among the accounts. All of them mention the empty tomb, the women who visit the tomb, the encounter of the women with angelic-type beings and Jesus' appearances to the disciples under a variety of circumstances. It is not so easy to see how all the details fit together; it is, however, easy to see that there are many more similarities than differences and that there is little that appears directly contradictory.

Here we have looked only at the charge of contradiction in the narratives of Jesus' resurrection. We will look in more detail below at the positive reasons for believing that the resurrection actually occurred.

The resurrection is a most unusual event. It probably has happened only once in the history of the entire world. To be sure, it is odd. But the resurrection becomes much less odd in light of who Jesus thought and showed himself to be while he was alive. If he was who he claimed to be, then his resurrection becomes if not intrinsically likely at least rationally consistent. Indeed, if anyone were ever to defy death, it would be a man like him.

Jesus According to the Gospels

The fifth and sixth reasons for skepticism are best treated together.

Reason 5 casts doubt on the Gospel writers' memories and reason 6 on their motivation. How can we evaluate these at the distance of two thousand years? This might seem impossible to do. Still, historians do it all the time.

First, it is well to dispel one common error still made by skeptics, the notion that the Gospels were written a long time after the events they record. Errors of this kind have a long life. In the nineteenth century some scholars did hold that the Gospels were not written until nearly a hundred years after the events they record. But this error has long been laid to rest by scholars in the twentieth century. The majority of modern scholars date Mark, generally thought to be the first Gospel, to the period of A.D. 65-70 (at least before the fall of Jerusalem in A.D. 70).[13] There is less agreement on the dating of Matthew and Luke, though the majority of scholars agree that they were written after Mark and before the end of the first century. Luke, for example, has been dated as early as the early 60s but seldom later that the 90s.[14] One scholar, J. A. T. Robinson, has even dated all of the New Testament before A.D. 70.[15] This includes the Gospel of John, which most scholars believe dates to A.D. 90-110. The upshot is that the Gospels began to circulate during the lifetime of people who were living at the time of the events of Jesus' life. The Gospels would never have achieved their status as authoritative documents in the church had they been challenged by such eyewitnesses.

In historical research, the general rule is to take the documents under consideration at face value unless there is telling reason to do otherwise. In other words, the burden of proof that the documents are unreliable resides with the skeptic. After all, if one finds, for example, a document claiming to be a letter from "Democritus" to "Damocles" and it has all the earmarks of other documents already considered authentic from the same period and the same general setting, then in all likelihood it is indeed a letter from Democritus to Damocles.

Take the Gospel of Luke. It opens with a statement of its purpose:
Many have undertaken to draw up an account of the things that have been fulfilled among us, just as they were handed down to us

by those who from the first were eyewitnesses and servants of the word. Therefore, since I myself have carefully investigated everything from the beginning, it seemed good also to me to write an orderly account for you, most excellent Theophilus, so that you may know the certainty of the things you have been taught. (Luke 1:1-4) The writer's claim is to be making an orderly account of material that derives directly from eyewitnesses. He is not an eyewitness, but his sources are. There is no hint here that he is doing anything contrary to recounting a series of events he believes to have occurred. In modern parlance, he says he is telling it like it was.

Of course, what a first-century writer thinks is important or interesting may be quite different from what we might think is important. Luke does not, for example, tell us anything about Jesus from age twelve to about age thirty. After the birth narratives, Jesus bursts on the scene as a mature teacher, prophet and healer. For Luke the intervening years were not important.

As readers we are always at the mercy of the authors we read. They determine what they want us to know. Examining a document to see what is there and what is not there can, in fact, suggest to us *why* we are being told what we are being told. The Gospels, for example, tell us much more about the final week in Jesus' life than about any other comparable time period. Why is that? Is it not, at least as far as the Gospel writers are concerned, that the supreme meaning of Jesus' life lies in what he did and said in that final week? That is what the church has always thought. The death and resurrection of Jesus are celebrated in the Eucharist every Sunday (sometimes even more often) by many Christian churches throughout the world from the time of Jesus to today.

The point here, however, is this: the fact that we do not have a massively detailed account of Jesus' life, death and resurrection is no reason to doubt that what we do have in the Gospel accounts is essentially accurate. The idea that the Gospel writers could not have known enough to be accurate or had motives that colored their accounts enough to make them historically unreliable is, before we take a look at what they actually wrote and the way they wrote it, simply prejudice.[16]

We must, then, look at the Gospels themselves. What do they say about Jesus? If Jesus is indeed the best reason for believing the Christian faith is true, let us examine the evidence.

The person and work of Christ are the rock upon which
the Christian religion is built. . . . Take Christ from Christianity,
and you disembowel it; there is practically nothing left.
Christ is the center of Christianity; all else is circumference.

JOHN STOTT, *BASIC CHRISTIANITY*

———————

Jesus
the
Reason

8

T he Gospel writers do not take long in getting to their subject—
the character of Jesus and his teaching, his healing, his death
and resurrection. The Gospel of Mark is the clearest example of
this. In a few bold strokes Mark sets the background for Jesus' entry
and then quickly brings him on stage.

The Dramatic Entrance of Jesus
Mark starts by quoting from the Hebrew Scriptures. They had foretold
a coming messenger who would prepare the way for "the Lord." Mark
identifies this messenger as John the Baptist, who came with a message of judgment, repentance and forgiveness. John's main work,
however, was to baptize Jesus and thus provide the context in which
Jesus was identified by a voice from heaven as God's Son. Mark then
says Jesus spent forty days in the desert being tempted by Satan. For
Mark this is all prologue—short, succinct, programmatic. In fact, Mark
dismisses John the Baptist's own tragic story of arrest by Herod by

placing it in a dependent clause introducing Jesus: "After John was put in prison, Jesus . . ." (Mark 1:14).

What comes next is public, dramatic and staggering in its implications. All the Gospels portray an astounding person, one who at every step does and says the unexpected. If any title ever fit this most unusual person, it would be The Unexpected Jesus; this theme resonates throughout the accounts of his life.

As Jesus enters the public arena, Mark says, he went into Galilee (northern Israel, where he was raised), "proclaiming the good news of God. 'The time has come,' he said. 'The kingdom of God is near. Repent and believe the good news!' " (1:14-15). Then immediately Mark shows Jesus calling disciples, driving out an evil spirit, healing Peter's mother-in-law, disappearing early in the morning to pray, healing a man with leprosy and generally gaining a reputation as a man who acts and speaks with authority. Mark describes the reaction of the people:

> The people were all so amazed that they asked each other, "What is this? A new teaching—and with authority! He even gives orders to evil spirits and they obey him." News about him spread quickly over the whole region of Galilee. (1:27-28)

We cannot examine every story the Synoptic Gospel writers tell. In fact, I will select only one from Mark and two from Luke. I will then look at one of Jesus' parables and a couple of his comments near the end of his life. In all, we will be heading toward one end: answering the question, Who is Jesus? The answer, we will see, will be immediately relevant to our ultimate goal: to determine whether Christianity is true.

A Man Through the Roof

One of the most interesting events that gave rise to the people's amazement is the story of four men who brought a crippled friend to Jesus. Let's hear it as Mark tells it.

> A few days later, when Jesus again entered Capernaum, the people heard that he had come home. So many gathered that there was

no room left, not even outside the door, and he preached the word to them. Some men came, bringing to him a paralytic, carried by four of them. Since they could not get him to Jesus because of the crowd, they made an opening in the roof above Jesus and, after digging through it, lowered the mat the paralyzed man was lying on. When Jesus saw their faith, he said to the paralytic, "Son, your sins are forgiven."

Now some teachers of the law were sitting there, thinking to themselves, "Why does this fellow talk like that? He's blaspheming! Who can forgive sins but God alone?"

Immediately Jesus knew in his spirit that this was what they were thinking in their hearts, and he said to them, "Why are you thinking these things? Which is easier: to say to the paralytic, 'Your sins are forgiven,' or to say, 'Get up, take your mat and walk'? But that you may know that the Son of Man has authority on earth to forgive sins . . . ." He said to the paralytic, "I tell you, get up, take your mat and go home." He got up, took his mat and walked out in full view of them all. This amazed everyone and they praised God, saying, "We have never seen anything like this!" (Mark 2:1-12)

This story has a number of unexpected twists. Each of them points to who Jesus is, or at least who he is claiming he is. First, Mark sets the scene—Jesus in a house in Capernaum, a city in northern Israel only some twenty miles from his hometown, Nazareth. By the time of the event narrated, Jesus had become famous, and lots of people were crowded into the house, including some teachers of the law. Luke tells us in a parallel account that "Pharisees and teachers of the law" had come from all over the surrounding area and from as far away as Judea and Jerusalem (Luke 5:17). Four men bent on getting their friend to Jesus so he could be healed proceeded directly to the unexpected. They opened up the roof of the house and let their paralytic friend down in front of Jesus.

Mark's account is spare. The bustle, the dust, the "what's going on here!" from the crowd inside are not mentioned, but we easily call up these images as we read the account. What Mark tells us is that the men lowered the paralytic through the roof so that he lay on his pallet on the floor before Jesus.

What was he there for? To be healed, of course. Did Jesus know that? Of course he did. So did he say, "I heal you in the name of the Lord God"? Not at all.

Rather, he said, "Son, your sins are forgiven" (bearing the force of "I forgive your sins").

Had the man's paralysis been a direct effect of the man's sins? Or did Jesus simply go directly to the man's deepest problem—not his paralysis but his status as a sinner before God?

Whatever is the case, the teachers of the law—experts in such religious matters—immediately saw a problem. Jesus did too. He knew what they were thinking. They had jumped right over the man's as-yet-unaddressed physical problem to a serious breach of orthodox theology. Jesus had proclaimed forgiveness for sins. Only God can do that.

Well, aren't they right about this? Let's see the issue in human terms first. Who can forgive a fault? Imagine, for example, that I kick my friend John in the shin and he begins to bleed so that he needs to be taken to a doctor.

My pastor, Bill, sees what I have done, and he comes over to me within John's hearing and says, "Gosh, Jim, that was a pretty bad thing to do. But I forgive you." Does Bill have the authority to forgive me? How could he? Only the one offended has the authority to forgive the offender. Only John can forgive me.

But had the paralytic offended Jesus? Not unless Jesus is much more than the man we see standing over the paralytic. After all, who is offended by sin? Is it not God? Even if I "sin" against John by kicking him and he forgives me, there is one whose forgiveness I yet need, for God did not want me to kick John. I have damaged some of God's property, someone he has made in his image. For that damage even John cannot forgive me. I need John's forgiveness if I am to be reconciled to John and God's forgiveness if I am to be reconciled with God.

It is in this sense that God alone can forgive sins. The teachers of the law were right.

But one more point should be seen. It has to do with why the forgiveness is given. Let's return to my kicking John. Suppose I feel bad about this so I say, "Gee, John, I'm sorry." Must John forgive me if I ask? That is, does my asking John for forgiveness *require* him to forgive me?

Of course not. He may or may not forgive me. It's his prerogative.

Let's say that I offer him my credit card and say, "Here, go to the doctor. He'll take care of you and charge my account." Now *must* he forgive me? Again no.

So then I offer him ten thousand dollars from my liability insurance. Now *must* he forgive me? Another no.

The fact is, any action I take, anything I say, does not force John to forgive me. It's up to him. If he forgives me, he does so freely. To be sure, if he is to act as God acts toward us, he will forgive me. But there is no necessity about it.

All of this stands behind Jesus' words to the paralytic: I forgive your sins because I have the authority to do so. You have committed sins not against me, the Jesus standing before you, but against God himself. Yet I can say, "Your sins are forgiven," and they are!

No wonder the teachers of the law were perturbed. To say what Jesus said, to claim what Jesus claimed, is to put oneself in the position of God. That's blasphemy.

Jesus easily knew what they were thinking (he did not even need superhuman power to do so; he could simply follow the normal pattern of Jewish religious thought). So he threw out a puzzler: "Is it easier to say, 'Your sins are forgiven,' or to say, 'Get up and walk'?" The implications of this question would not be lost on his audience. One could say either one just as easily. But which one could produce the effect required? Forgiven sins cannot be detected. Maybe one should say that. But that would be to blaspheme. Such a statement would itself need to be forgiven! So maybe one should say, "Get up and walk." But then one would have to be able to cure paralysis.

Jesus made the choice simple: he claimed to do both. "In order to show that I have the authority to forgive sins, I am going to heal this man." And he did. No wonder the people wondered!

And no wonder we wonder as well. What sort of man could have done and said what he did? Could it be that he was able to heal both body and soul? Our wonder continues as we read on in the Gospels.

Jesus in His Hometown

The next story comes from the Gospel of Luke. It is Luke's first narrative of Jesus in action. The event took place, Luke tells us, after Jesus had returned from the desert, where he was tempted, and after he had already taught in some of the synagogues in the region where he grew up. Luke says that the initial response to him was quite positive: "everyone praised him" (Luke 4:15). Now go on to the first part of Luke's account:

He went to Nazareth, where he had been brought up, and on the Sabbath day he went into the synagogue, as was his custom. And he stood up to read. The scroll of the prophet Isaiah was handed to him. Unrolling it, he found the place where it is written:

"The Spirit of the Lord is on me,
  because he has anointed me
  to preach good news to the poor.
He has sent me to proclaim freedom for the prisoners
  and recovery of sight for the blind,
to release the oppressed,
  to proclaim the year of the Lord's favor."

Then he rolled up the scroll, gave it back to the attendant and sat down. The eyes of everyone in the synagogue were fastened on him, and he began by saying to them, "Today this scripture is fulfilled in your hearing."

All spoke well of him and were amazed at the gracious words that came from his lips. "Isn't this Joseph's son?" they asked. (Luke 4:16-22)

As we read this today, we may be unaware of the radical nature of what Jesus has done here. But one thing we can well understand. Jesus has been gone from Nazareth for some time, at least forty days in the desert and some time after that teaching in synagogues in Galilee. Having been away from his hometown for a significant period, now he has returned.

Imagine that Phil Freshman, a college student, comes home for the first time after entering the university a few months before. On Sunday he goes to the church he grew up in, and the pastor says, "Phil, why don't you read the Scripture for the day?"

Phil says, "Sure," and then proceeds to find a text in the Prophets and reads it. When he closes the Bible, he says, "You see this task that the prophet says he has come to perform. That task is mine. I am the one who will really fulfill this prophecy. I am the one all of Israel has been looking for."

Can you see the folk in the congregation? They look at each other. They smile. At first they think, *Hey, this kid is really something. They must have taught him a lot at school. He really has spunk.* Then it hits them. *Wait a minute. Who does Phil think he is? Isn't this Frank the contractor's son? What's going on here?*

Jesus, as Luke explains, knew what the people in the Nazareth congregation were thinking. So the story continues:

Jesus said to them, "Surely you will quote this proverb to me: 'Physician, heal yourself! Do here in your hometown what we have heard that you did in Capernaum.' "

"I tell you the truth," he continued, "no prophet is accepted in his hometown. I assure you that there were many widows in Israel in Elijah's time, when the sky was shut for three and a half years and there was a severe famine throughout the land. Yet Elijah was not sent to any of them, but to a widow in Zarephath in the region of Sidon. And there were many in Israel with leprosy in the time of Elisha the prophet, yet not one of them was cleansed—only Naaman the Syrian."

All the people in the synagogue were furious when they heard this. They got up, drove him out of the town, and took him to the brow of the hill on which the town was built, in order to throw him down the cliff. But he walked right through the crowd and went on his way. (4:23-30)

Phil Freshman will probably not get far with the congregation of his home church if he announces himself as the fulfillment of biblical prophecy. They will think he is crazy or seriously deluded or pulling their leg.

Jesus did not let the people's reactions bother him. In fact, he added fuel to the fire.

He had already associated himself with one of their greatest prophets, Isaiah. Now he reminded them of two more, and he selected from their lives two incidents that focus attention on the people's failure to believe him. Elijah had helped a widow in the area that is now called Lebanon; she was not an Israelite. Elisha had healed a Syrian rather than an Israelite.[1] Now God was sending another of his servants to Israel, to the chosen people, to the hometown of the prophet himself, and the hometown Israelites were refusing to acknowledge him.

Essentially what Jesus is saying is that in the past God has at times ignored his own people and given his blessings to those who are not of the "chosen" race. Jesus is implying that if the people of Nazareth don't accept him as who he says he is, he will do the same thing. No wonder they are angry! More than angry—they act on their anger and try to get rid of him completely. But Jesus—perhaps by the sheer strength of his personality—simply walks through the crowd and goes on his way. Interestingly, we never hear of Jesus' returning to Nazareth.

As readers we, just as much as Jesus' Nazarene neighbors, again face a dilemma. Is Jesus who he said he was—the prophet described by Isaiah? Is he the one whose mission was to challenge the mores of the day: "preach good news to the poor . . . proclaim freedom for the prisoners and recovery of sight for the blind"? Did he "release the oppressed"? And most poignantly, did he "proclaim the year of the Lord's favor" (that is, did he inaugurate a community in which there would be a restoration of social justice)?[2] If we agree that he was who he said he was, then we need to align ourselves with him and take on his agenda. If we do not agree, we run the risk of being left behind as God through Jesus does his good work through others.

What is that good work that Jesus vows to do? Much of what Jesus meant by quoting Isaiah becomes clear as we follow Luke's account of what Jesus continued to do and say. He was constantly associating with the down and out—the poor, the lame, the sick, the hookers, the despised Jews who were collectors of Roman taxes. He healed those who were afflicted, he brought sight to the blind, he freed people not so much from their place in the social order as from the shame and stigma of being on the margins of society. He warned against the dangers of wealth and told stories in which the rich were shown to be poor and the poor to be rich. Not that he did not associate in any way with those in the middle and upper echelons of society. They too hung around Jesus, and he dined with them as well.

That brings us to the third story we will look at in detail.

The Woman Who Loved Much
The stories of Jesus as they are told in the Gospels are often laden with irony and paradox. The rich are poor; the up are down; the down are up; the self-righteous are sinners; the sinners are forgiven. In the following account we see Jesus in dialogue with both a man in the center of society and a woman on the margins.

> Now one of the Pharisees invited Jesus to have dinner with him, so he went to the Pharisee's house and reclined at the table. When a woman who had lived a sinful life in that town learned that Jesus was eating at the Pharisee's house, she brought an alabaster jar of perfume, and as she stood behind him at his feet weeping, she began to wet his feet with her tears. Then she wiped them with her hair, kissed them and poured perfume on them.
>
> When the Pharisee who had invited him saw this, he said to himself, "If this man were a prophet, he would know who is touching him and what kind of woman she is—that she is a sinner."

Jesus answered him, "Simon, I have something to tell you."

"Tell me, teacher," he said.

"Two men owed money to a certain moneylender. One owed him five hundred denarii, and the other fifty. Neither of them had the money to pay him back, so he canceled the debts of both. Now which of them will love him more?"

Simon replied, "I suppose the one who had the bigger debt canceled."

"You have judged correctly," Jesus said.

Then he turned toward the woman and said to Simon, "Do you see this woman? I came into your house. You did not give me any water for my feet, but she wet my feet with her tears and wiped them with her hair. You did not give me a kiss, but this woman, from the time I entered, has not stopped kissing my feet. You did not put oil on my head, but she has poured perfume on my feet. Therefore, I tell you, her many sins have been forgiven—for she loved much. But he who has been forgiven little loves little."

Then Jesus said to her, "Your sins are forgiven."

The other guests began to say among themselves, "Who is this who even forgives sins?"

Jesus said to the woman, "Your faith has saved you; go in peace." (Luke 7:36-50)

The scene is graphically portrayed and needs little comment. Suffice it to say that a normal social occasion—Jesus' dining with a devoted Jewish keeper of the law—was interrupted by a party-crasher. Into the home of an upstanding citizen of the community came, uninvited, a woman everyone would know as a prostitute. What was she doing there? Shocking enough was her presence; more shocking still was what she did to Jesus. Taking expensive oil—probably purchased from the proceeds of her business—she anointed Jesus' feet and wiped them with her long hair.

Simon was appalled. *How can this "holy man" who heals and gives such profoundly ethical teaching allow this to happen?* Jesus knew what was running through Simon's mind, and he responded by doing what he did better than anyone before or after him: he told a story that implicated the audience in the telling. He gave Simon a choice: "Who loves the most—the one forgiven a smaller debt or a larger debt?"

Notice the reticence, perhaps the tone of disgust, in Simon's "I *suppose.*" Simon was saying, in effect, "Well, of course—what a stupid question! Are you insulting me with it? It's the one whose debt was largest."

Then came Jesus' unexpected commendation and condemnation all at the same time: "You're right. Here I am, a guest in your home. You've offered me the bare minimum of hospitality, but not so much as to show that you really care much about me. In fact, I suspect you are having *me* for lunch!"

Then he turned to the woman and recognized all the honor she had given him. "Why has she done this?" Jesus asked. "Because she loves me much—very much. She knows who she is—a sinner—and she knows she has been forgiven.

"And you, Simon?" At this point Simon himself has been had for lunch. For whether Simon caught on or not, we do. Simon is the sinner who doesn't know it. Simon is unforgiven.

Again, those around were baffled: Who is this who can forgive such sins as those of this poor woman? We might add, Who is this who sees with such clarity! And who is this who tells such clever stories!

Jesus' final word to the woman was the great comfort he gives to all who know who they are and come to him for reconciliation with God. As Matthew quotes Jesus in his Gospel: "Come to me, all you who are weary and burdened, and I will give you rest. Take my yoke upon you and learn from me, for I am gentle and humble in heart, and you will find rest for your souls. For my yoke is easy and my burden is light" (11:28-30).

The Outlines of a Portrait
Just from the three passages we have looked at, the outlines of a portrait of Jesus are beginning to emerge: He inaugurated in a special way the longed-for kingdom of God. He announced his intention to

fulfill the Hebrew prophecy of a man who would be given a special task of reconciling people with people and people with God. He inspired awe and shock, upset normal expectations, forgave the sins of those who knew themselves as sinners, cleverly prodded the self-righteous to recognize their sinfulness, walked among the ordinary people and challenged them to join him in bringing the kingdom of God into the highways and the byways of life.

It may seem far-fetched to suggest that a penniless preacher
from a rural backwater of the Roman Empire offers us the key to
the understanding of the purposes of God in human history.
It may seem even more incredible to claim that he was and is
the divine Son of God, the ultimate revelation to his creatures.
Yet millions of apparently sane and intelligent people today do
make those claims, as did his first followers.

DAVID WINTER, *TRUTH IN THE SON*

————

Jesus:
The Dilemma
of His
Identity

9

The evidence for who Jesus really was (or is!) is rich in detail, far richer than most people who have not looked into it ever imagine. The Gospels are short. Each one can be read in a single sitting. But in the briefest compass they record events and sayings that penetrate deeply into the character of their chief figure.

In this chapter we will examine two brief passages that point up for us a troubling challenge: Is Jesus who he thought he was? That's the intellectual belief issue. Are we ready to act on what we come to believe is true about him? That's the life issue. Belief and action are bound inextricably together. That's what makes the Christian religion so hard to deal with.

Teacher and Storyteller

We have just seen how Jesus responded to an unconventional situation—an outsider's invasion of an insider's home. We look now at a more ordinary situation in which there again arises the opportunity for Jesus to teach by telling a story. Here is Luke's description of the setting.

> On one occasion an expert in the law stood up to test Jesus. "Teacher," he asked, "what must I do to inherit eternal life?"
>
> "What is written in the Law?" he replied. "How do you read it?"
>
> He answered: " 'Love the Lord your God with all your heart and with all your soul and with all your strength and with all your mind'; and, 'Love your neighbor as yourself.' "
>
> "You have answered correctly," Jesus replied. "Do this and you will live."
>
> But he wanted to justify himself, so he asked Jesus, "And who is my neighbor?" (Luke 10:25-29)

As Jesus traveled and taught, he was often asked questions, and just as often he asked them. That's the case here. The opening question was a big one: "What must I do to be so approved by God that I may live forever, including having life after death?"

Jesus responded with a question: "What do you think? You're an expert in the law. You tell me. What does the law say?"

The lawyer then responded by quoting from two sections of the Hebrew Scriptures: "One must love God with everything one is and one's neighbor as oneself" (see Deuteronomy 6:5 and Leviticus 19:18 for the original texts).

"This is technically correct," Jesus replied. "Now go do it."

Luke gives us a hint as to what is running through the lawyer's mind. He has already told us that the original question he was asking was a poser; it was designed to "test Jesus." It is obvious that the test is going poorly, not for Jesus but for the lawyer. Jesus has put him on record. The man knows what God requires—total devotion to him and a selfless servant attitude to others. When Jesus simply challenges him to do what he knows to do, be what he knows he ought to be, he is caught in a bind. He realizes that he is not making the grade, even by the standards he believes to be right. So he asks another question: "Okay. So who is my neighbor?"

Jesus then tells one of his simplest yet most powerful stories.

In reply Jesus said: "A man was going down from Jerusalem to Jericho, when he fell into the hands of robbers. They stripped him of his clothes, beat him and went away, leaving him half dead. A priest happened to be going down the same road, and when he saw the man, he passed by on the other side. So too, a Levite, when he came to the place and saw him, passed by on the other side. But a Samaritan, as he traveled, came where the man was; and when he saw him, he took pity on him. He went to him and bandaged his wounds, pouring on oil and wine. Then he put the man on his own donkey, took him to an inn and took care of him. The next day he took out two silver coins and gave them to the innkeeper. 'Look after him,' he said, 'and when I return, I will reimburse you for any extra expense you may have.' " (Luke 10:30-35)

After the story, Jesus poses his second question:

"Which of these three do think was a neighbor to the man who fell into the hands of robbers?"

The expert in the law replied, "The one who had mercy on him."

Jesus told him, "Go and do likewise." (10:36-37)

Again, the expert in the law knew the answer. Actually it is so simple that any child who heard the story would know. But the implications for the lawyer were profound. He had to *do* what he knew. He had to act. Jesus has charged him to be responsible to his knowledge.

Notice, however, that Jesus in the story did not actually answer the lawyer's question. The expert had asked, "Who is my neighbor?" Jesus in effect said, "That is the wrong question. The point is not to figure out whether you must love only your fellow Jews or whether you must draw the circle larger and include the aliens in the land or the Roman occupation forces. The point is to *be* a neighbor. If you *are* a neighbor, then you act neighborly toward anyone who needs you as a neighbor."

This point is brought home forcefully by the characters in the story. It is a Jew who is in a ditch, and it is Jews, very religious law-keeping ones, who leave the Jew in the ditch. It is a hated Samaritan who does what is right.[1] Jesus, much as he did in Nazareth, has made the outsider the hero in the story. How this must have galled the expert in the law!

Imagine the scene today. If Jesus were to tell the same story to a Christian lawyer, it would be a very orthodox pastor and a very scrupulously religious elder who walked by the man. The neighbor would have been a Moonie or a Hindu or a Buddhist. And it would gall the Christian audience. Does it not offend me as I write this? But then it should dawn on us that Jesus is right: those who do God's work in the world include some whose theology is not orthodox. Does it mean they inherit eternal life? That is more than can be said from this passage. The point rather is that some non-Jews (for us, some non-followers of Jesus) have the character we should have and do what we should be doing.

But let's return to the lawyer. *Could* he do what he knew he must do? *Could* he love God totally and his neighbor as himself? Surely the expert must realize that that is impossible. Has Jesus then set for him an impossible task and thus condemned him to a loss of eternal life? These questions can only be answered as we see Jesus' teaching elsewhere in the Gospels. We have already seen, however, what Jesus showed Simon the Pharisee: that those who know themselves to be sinners can be forgiven, and that it is out of forgiveness that love for God comes. The one who is forgiven much loves much.

Did the lawyer realize he was a sinner? It would seem so. But so far that knowledge had led only to his attempt to "justify himself." Would he and Simon ever see themselves as sinners? Luke does not tell us. In fact, many of Jesus' stories leave us hanging.[2] They are open-ended.

Even we who overhear the stories are put on record. Do *we* love God totally? Do *we* love our neighbor? For anyone with self-knowledge, the answer is obvious. So what must we do? Again the answer is obvious: we must confess that sin and turn to Jesus for forgiveness. If we do, we will be forgiven; we will inherit eternal life.

But—and here is where the argument for the truth of the Christian faith meets a barrier—we are responsible for what we know. If Jesus is right, we will have to change our attitude, recognize our sinfulness, confess this before God and trust in Jesus to forgive us. That is simple to understand but very hard to do. Yet that is what is at stake when we search for the truth. If it turns out that Jesus is who he thought himself to be—at this point in our analysis, a teacher of the way to eternal life and a forgiver of sins—then we can't let what we know be only "intellectual." A personal response is required.

Is Christianity true? is directly related to *Will I obey the truth?*

It is at this point that many turn away. *If Jesus is right,* they reason, *I want none of it.* Rejecting Christianity is, then, a matter not so much of rejecting what one knows is false as of rejecting what one strongly suspects is true but costs too much to accept. Anticipating just such a situation, Jesus once said, "If anyone would come after me, he must deny himself and take up his cross and follow me. For whoever wants to save his life will lose it, but whoever loses his life for me and for the gospel will save it" (Mark 8:34-35).

This is a breathtaking demand: to follow Jesus is to leave your own goals and aspirations behind and take up the agenda of Jesus, live for the kingdom of God. But as Jesus pointed out, the choice to follow Jesus still makes the most sense: "What good is it for a man to gain the whole world, yet forfeit his soul? Or what can a man give in exchange for his soul?" (Mark 8:36-37).

We can add one more line to the emerging sketch of Jesus. Jesus is one who tells clever stories, implicates the hearer in the tale and forces a decision. He is one who even steps out of the pages of the Gospels, implicates the reader and forces a decision.

Is Jesus who he thinks he is? On the answer to this question rides the truth of the Christian faith and the glory or futility of the Christian life.

There is one more text we need to consider in some detail. It concerns one of the last things Jesus did and said before his crucifixion.

The Last Supper

All of the Gospels tell the story of the last week of Jesus' life. I will focus on only one detail of that story—the "last" meal Jesus ate with his disciples. The meal itself was a celebration of the Passover—the annual reminder of the exodus, the escape of the Hebrew people from slavery in Egypt a thousand or so years before. The Passover feast was filled with stylized symbolism, each element of the meal signifying a part of the story. The Jews were, for example, to eat only unleavened bread (bread made without yeast) because at the time of the exodus there was no time for the bread to rise before the people had to escape.

During the last meal with his disciples, Jesus chose to focus on this bread and on the wine. Here is Luke's account in chapter 22:

> When the hour came, Jesus and his apostles reclined at the table. And he said to them, "I have eagerly desired to eat this Passover with you before I suffer. For I tell you, I will not eat it again until it finds fulfillment in the kingdom of God."
>
> After taking the cup, he gave thanks and said, "Take this and divide it among you. For I tell you I will not drink again of the fruit of the vine until the kingdom of God comes."
>
> And he took bread, gave thanks and broke it, and gave it to them, saying, "This is my body given for you; do this in remembrance of me."
>
> In the same way, after the supper he took the cup, saying, "This cup is the new covenant in my blood, which is poured out for you." (vv. 14-19)

After this he pointed out that there was one person at the meal (it would turn out to be Judas) who was going to betray him. This meal, the Last Supper, was indeed a solemn occasion, and it has ever since been celebrated wherever there are Christians.[3] The very essence of the meaning of Jesus' life and death is contained in the rite. I will not begin to plumb the depth of the meaning of the Last Supper here.[4] The point is what it tells us about who Jesus thought he was. To understand that, we need to understand more about the Passover feast.

In Jesus' day, each Jewish family brought a lamb to the temple. After it was ritually slain, the meat was cooked for the Passover feast. This sacrifice reenacted an event in Egypt just prior to the exodus. Moses had been pleading with Pharaoh to allow the Hebrews to leave Egypt to return to Canaan, the land God had promised to Abraham and his descendants. In a last effort to secure their release, Moses told Pharaoh that on a certain date the firstborn of each family in Egypt would be slain by the angel of death unless he released the Hebrews. There were two ways this terrible judgment could be avoided: Pharaoh could release the Hebrews, or the Egyptians could come under the Hebrews' protection. Each Hebrew family was to sacrifice a lamb and smear some of the blood on the doorposts of their houses. When the angel of death passed through, he would "pass over" the marked houses of the Hebrews and spare all who had sought protection within.

Pharaoh refused to let the Israelites go, and the angel of death took the lives of many Egyptians. That was the final blow to Pharaoh. He released the Israelites. Thus the annual remembrance in the Feast of the Passover.

By Jesus' time, Passover had for years been interpreted not just as a memory of the past but as a hope for the future, a time when God would again free the Jews from their oppressor—this time not Egypt but Rome. Jesus took this celebration, gave it a radically different interpretation and showed what its ultimate meaning really was. For him the Passover feast pointed to the sacrifice that he was going to make the very next day by dying. "This is my body," he said of the broken bread. "This cup is the new covenant in my blood, which is poured out for you." That is, "A new 'covenant'—a new agreement—is being made between God and you," he was saying to his disciples. "And it all has to do with the sacrifice I will be making tomorrow—the innocent (like a lamb) slain for the guilty."

There is so much more that could be said. I could note that in the Passover feast there were four cups of wine, each having a different significance. Jesus drank the third cup, the cup of redemption. He did not drink the fourth cup, the cup of consummation, for this will only be drunk when he "eats with redeemed sinners in the Kingdom of

God."[5] In refusing the fourth cup, he was foreshadowing his Second Coming and his reign as King of kings and Lord of lords beyond the end of history.

We could also examine in depth the close connection between the Last Supper and Jesus' cry of dereliction on the cross: "My God, my God, why have you forsaken me?" (Mark 15:34). Here Jesus was quoting the opening verse of Psalm 22 and was taking into himself all the agony of sinful Israel, dying as a substitute for all Israel and all humankind. We could see too the connection to the prophecy of the Suffering Servant in Isaiah 53 and to Jesus' words earlier in Mark: "For even the Son of Man did not come to be served, but to serve, and to give his life as a ransom for many" (Mark 10:45). Wrapped up in the eucharistic words—"This is my body; this is my blood"—is the self-understanding of a man who saw himself to be the final sacrifice for the sins of humankind.

So again we add to our sketch of Jesus. Here was a man who saw himself not only as having the power and authority to forgive sins but also as the sacrifice by which God's forgiveness would be possible.

Facing Up to the Consequences

We could fill in the sketch we have seen of Jesus until many more details became clear. If we examined the Gospels fully, we could in fact come up with a full-color portrait. Still, even with the hasty sketch I have drawn, enough of the facts are now before us, at least enough to see how the argument works.

Put in its simplest form, the argument goes like this: Either Jesus was who he thought and said he was or he was not. If he was who he thought and said he was, then Christianity is true. If he was not who he thought and said he was, then he was either a liar or so deluded as to be a lunatic. He was neither a liar nor a lunatic. Therefore, Jesus was who he said he was, and Christianity is true.[6]

In this short form, the argument looks too simple to be valid. We need to look at the details that back it up.

Take the first possibility. What if Jesus was right about who he was?

This horn of the dilemma is not difficult to understand. Jesus thought of himself as teaching the truth about God, about people and about the world around us. If he was who he thought and said he was, then Christianity is true.

It also follows that Christianity is *not* first and foremost a theological or philosophical system. It is primarily a way of life centering on a personal relationship with God through Jesus Christ. If Jesus is who he thought he was, then our proper response is not just to believe him but also to obey him: to confess who we are, people broken and in need of forgiveness, to place our trust in him as our Savior and to follow him as our Lord. The truth of Christianity requires no less.

But what of the other horn of the dilemma: that Jesus is not who he thought he was or who he pretended to be? That horn leads to another dilemma and two more horns. Jesus would then be either a liar or so deluded about himself as to be insane.

Could Jesus have been a liar? To this (if the Gospels are giving us an accurate picture of who Jesus was) it is easy to say no. There is simply no evidence that Jesus did not think he was telling the truth. He taught with a sense of great personal authority; everyone, even those who did not believe him, noticed that. He presented a consistent picture of God, himself and others. When liars elaborate or answer the same kinds of questions repeatedly, they are easily caught in inconsistencies. There is in Jesus a unity of teaching: the stories, the clever sayings, the constant compassion for people, the obvious wisdom of his teaching, the ethical depth of both his teaching and his character. No fault could be found in him. At his trial, his accusers contradicted themselves, but Jesus stood at his trial with the same integrity as he did on city streets.

The most telling reason for Jesus' not being a liar is that if he was lying, he was lying about the most important issues of life: how to please God, how to inherit eternal life, how to be blessed, how to live well among both your friends and your enemies. If he was lying, he would be selling a salvation he knew to be fake. In fact, he would be no better than the worst religious huckster we know of today, no better than Bhagwan Shree Rajneesh or Jim Jones or David Koresh. No one can call the Jesus of the Gospels that kind of bad man. It fits with none of the evidence whatsoever.

Let's examine the second horn. Maybe Jesus was right about a lot of things—how to respond to enemies, how to get along well in life—but wrong about who he was. Maybe he wasn't the one who could forgive sins or the one who died as a "ransom for many" (Mark 10:45). He just thought he was.

The problem here is that this kind of delusion is no small matter. This is a delusion about ultimate concerns. Jesus was claiming, if not to be God, at least to stand in the place of God. He was claiming a special relation to God such that those who follow him are saved and those who don't are not. At the least this is religious megalomania. True, early in his ministry his words and actions were strange enough that his own family once thought he might be "out of his mind" (Mark 3:21). But we never hear of this again, and given the fact that Jesus' brother James became one of the leaders of the early church, we may be confident that his family's worry was not long-lived.

The fact is that religious megalomania is usually accompanied by paranoia—a fear of those outside one's own fold—and antisocial behavior. Take David Koresh. At least reportedly he claimed for himself some characteristics of Christ. He holed up in a compound for safety and stored weapons for what he took to be a coming cataclysm. Bhagwan Shree Rajneesh employed guards to protect himself and his community from what was probably only imagined danger. Jim Jones took his followers to a far-off compound, guarded by men with weapons. He sponsored a mass suicide. Jesus was like none of these.

Nor was he like the people in mental institutions who believe themselves to be Christ. These people are unable to cope with ordinary life. Nobody believes them, not even others in the institution.

There is, of course, the possibility of a parallel to the charge of insanity: perhaps Jesus was demon-possessed. This is not the sort of charge that most modern readers would make, but it certainly was a possibility in the worldview of the people of Jesus' day. Jesus just did not fit into the ordinary categories of his own time. While there were other charismatic holy men in Israel who could cast out demons, Jesus stood in a class by himself. He was so successful that some teachers of the law, wondering how he could have so much power over demons, said, "He is possessed by Beelzebub! By the prince of demons he is driving out demons" (Mark 3:22).

But Jesus pointed out that this is impossible: "How can Satan drive out Satan? If a kingdom is divided against itself, that kingdom cannot stand. And if Satan opposes himself and is divided, he cannot stand; his end has come" (vv. 23-26). Then Jesus went even further: "whoever blasphemes against the Holy Spirit will never be forgiven; he is guilty of an eternal sin" (v. 29). In short, Jesus showed that their accusation of demon possession was not only illogical but spiritually dangerous. By saying this Jesus was claiming to cast out demons by the power of the Holy Spirit. To call a work of the Holy Spirit a work of the devil is spiritually deadly.[7]

In short, Jesus gave every appearance of being a psychologically normal person who so surprised people with what he did and said that it took a long time to figure out who he really was. Psychologist John A. Sanford uses C. G. Jung's categories of personality to investigate Jesus, concluding that he was balanced in every way: extravert-introvert, thinking-feeling, sensation-intuition, masculine-feminine. Moreover, he had a strong and healthy ego. Listen to Sanford's comments about Jesus' sanity:

> Looked at psychologically, the Gospels reveal the personality of a whole person. It is apparent that we have here in Jesus of Nazareth the paradigm of a whole person, the prototype of all human development, a truly individual person, and therefore someone unique.[8]

Sanford goes on to argue that the personality and character of the Jesus who emerges from the Gospels are themselves an argument for his actual historical existence:

> The personality and teachings of Jesus are not inherited from the collective spirit of his time, but stand out in contrast to it. Their very

uniqueness is a testimony to the reality of his personhood. . . . Such a personality must have existed, for he could never have been invented.[9]

Such a person is more likely to know who he is than any of the rest of us. If he is mad, then we are far madder yet.

The Case So Far

Where have we come in this long argument about who Jesus is? Just here: If Jesus is who he thought and said he was, Christianity is true. The best explanation for Jesus is that he is who he thought he was. So Christianity has a major claim to be considered true.

Is the case closed, the truth of the Christian faith proved absolutely? No. We never have that level of philosophic certitude about any religious or philosophical claim. But we do have good reason for thinking Christianity is in fact true. We do not need to throw our brains out the window to be disciples of Jesus.

We have not examined all the evidence that points to who Jesus was and is, but we have seen the pattern of that evidence. When the Gospels are considered in depth, the outlines of the pattern are filled in, and the evidence for the truth of the Christian faith is seen to be very strong indeed. There are, of course, other patterns of reason to follow.

Some skepticism about the accuracy of the picture of Jesus may, however, still haunt us. Is Jesus really the person we have seen him to be in this and the previous chapter? Haven't some recent scholars given us a quite different view of Jesus? Indeed they have. Some of those views, and reasons to refine or reject them, we will examine in the following chapter. Since the argument for Jesus as the "best reason" for believing the Christian faith rests on our knowing who Jesus is, this aspect of the discussion is vital.

Of course I had a deep respect, indeed a great reverence for the conventional Jesus Christ whom the Church worshipped. But I was not at all prepared for the *unconventional* man revealed in these terse Gospels. No one could possibly have invented such a person: this was no puppet-hero built out of the imaginations of adoring admirers. "This man Jesus" so briefly described, rang true, sometimes alarmingly true. I began to see now why the religious Establishment of those days wanted to get rid of him at all costs. He was sudden death to pride, pomposity and pretence.

J. B. PHILLIPS, *THE RING OF TRUTH*

———

The
Scholars'
Quest
for Jesus
10

T he identity of Jesus is crucial to the Christian faith. There is
nothing more central to the assessment of the truth of Christianity. If we can't know who Jesus really was or is, Jesus can be
neither the center of Christianity nor a reason for anyone to believe
the Christian vision of the reality of the God of Abraham, Isaac and
Jacob and the Father of Jesus Christ. Any skepticism about whether
we can know accurately who Jesus is must be resolved.

There are two ways to use and respond to this skepticism: (1) to
examine the uniqueness of Jesus in his time and (2) to examine the
similarity of Jesus to his time. The first involves certain *criteria of
authenticity;* the second involves intense historical study of the social
scene contemporary with Jesus.[1] The first gives us Jesus the Unique;
the second Jesus the Man of His Time. Properly understood, they are
not mutually exclusive.

Criteria of Authenticity

Since the Enlightenment, belief in the notion of a God who is personally concerned for his creation has waned. For over a century, naturalism, the notion that the cosmos exists solely on its own without having been created or sustained in existence by God, has been the dominant mindset of the university world. No wonder doubt has been cast on the historicity of the Gospels! But what kind of sketch can be drawn of Jesus if one removes the miraculous from the picture?

A number of attempts to see Jesus as solely human have been offered. The most interesting of the early "quests of the historical Jesus" are those by H. S. Reimarus (1694-1768), D. F. Strauss (1808-1874), Ernest Renan (1823-1892), H. J. Holzman (1832-1910) and Johannes Weiss (1863-1914).[2] Except for the general idea that Jesus was only human, the portraits drawn by these authors are no longer considered accurate. Albert Schweitzer in his monumental study *The Quest of the Historical Jesus* (1910) showed that "a great deal of writing about Jesus was simply imaginative fantasy."[3] Skeptical scholars were just seeing their own reflection in the face of Jesus.

Schweitzer himself depicted a Jesus who had failed in his mission, a mission Schweitzer took to be to bring in a transcendent kingdom of God within his lifetime. N. T. Wright, however, notes that this view turned out to be no less problematic:

> Schweitzer's sketch of Jesus was so unpalatable that a great many people refused to accept it. Since, however, it was apparently based on thorough historical scholarship, the only way that serious people could get round it was by denying that the question of "who Jesus really was" could have any great significance.[4]

The effect was to emphasize a schism between the Jesus of history (whom one could not know) and the Christ of faith (whom one believed in without knowing who the historical Jesus was). What then was called the Quest of the Historical Jesus was over.

It was not until the 1950s that a "New Quest" of the historical Jesus was launched, with various results, by such scholars as Ernst Käsemann, Günther Bornkamm, Edward Schillebeeckx and Joachim Jeremias.

Though the Jesus of Jeremias comes close, none of these scholars concluded that the Jesus of history was fully like the Jesus that we see in a straightforward reading of the Gospels.[5] But for highly skeptical readers of the Gospels today, one of the methods they used to construct the "historical Jesus" has merit. They developed a set of criteria to distinguish what they thought was historically authentic from what they suspected was contributed by or highly colored by the writers of the Gospels. The method applies not so much to what Jesus is said to have *done* as to what he is said to have *said.* There are four criteria of authenticity. I will examine only the first two and will do so in the form used by Norman Perrin, one of the most skeptical of modern scholars.

The first and most important criterion is the *criterion of dissimilarity:* "the earliest form of a saying we can reach may be regarded as authentic if it can be shown to be dissimilar to characteristic emphases both of ancient Judaism and of the early Church."[6] In other words, when Jesus is recorded as having said something that is unlike what any of his contemporaries or any of the early Christians are known to have said, then it is likely to be authentic.

The second criterion is the *criterion of coherence:* "material from the earliest strata of the tradition may be accepted as authentic if it can be shown to cohere with material established as authentic by means of the criterion of dissimilarity.'"[7] If, for example, an element of Jesus' sayings fits in with those sayings that pass the first criterion, then they too can be considered authentic.

What happens when the first of these criteria is applied to the sayings of Jesus? That depends on the somewhat subjective judgment of the scholar. But a great number of Jesus' sayings do not meet the criterion. Some critics have used the criterion of dissimilarity as a *principle of exclusion* and have concluded, on this basis, that any statement that does not meet the criterion is inauthentic. This is, of course, an utter misuse of the principle.

We should expect Jesus to have said many things that others said before him and that still others developed after him. After all, if Jesus said nothing that had been said by others of his time or in the Hebrew Scriptures, he would have been very odd indeed. Moreover, if he said nothing that his followers remembered and used in the early Christian community, then he could hardly be what his followers considered him, the Lord of their lives. The criterion of dissimilarity cannot, then, be used as a principle of exclusion. Many things that Jesus said must have been said by others as well.

If, however, the criterion is used only as a positive test of authenticity, a *principle of validation,* then it can have some value. It can show that it is reasonable to believe that Jesus made some particular statements. Some of the sayings that meet the criterion carry considerable freight in showing us who Jesus thought he was. We will examine one of them in some detail.

The Finger of God
Norman Perrin finds only a handful of sayings that meet the first criterion of dissimilarity, but one he deals with first and in considerable depth is revealing.

> But if it is by the finger of God that I cast out demons, then the Kingdom of God has come upon you. (Luke 11:20)[8]

The saying itself comes in a section of Luke in which Jesus has been accused of casting out demons by the power of Beelzebub, a name applied to the devil. As we saw in the previous chapter, Jesus responds by arguing that this is logically impossible: Satan would be destroying his own kingdom. If demons are to be cast out, it will be by the power of God, not Satan. Perrin notes that the phrase "finger of God" is an allusion to the story of the exodus. When Moses performed certain wonders to convince Pharaoh to allow the Hebrews to return to Palestine, Pharaoh's magicians were able to duplicate some of them. But Moses could bring forth lice (or gnats, some translations say) and the magicians couldn't. So they said to Pharaoh, "This is the finger of God" (Exodus 8:19). In a passage paralleling Luke's account of Jesus' argument about the source of his power, the phrase "finger of God" is replaced by "Spirit of God" (Matthew 12:28).

But Jesus goes further than claiming that it is the Spirit of God that is at work in his ministry of exorcism. He says that his exorcisms are manifestations of the kingdom of God. Perrin goes to considerable length to show just how the concept of the kingdom of God was central to Jesus' teaching. Then he demonstrates that this saying is not just characteristic of the words of Jesus throughout the Synoptic Gospels but also different from anything others were saying at the time and from any of the ways the early church later used the phrase. That is, Jesus' concept of the kingdm of God meets the criterion of dissimilarity.

So what does all this have to do with our argument about the truth of the Christian faith? Perrin himself does not seem to notice, but Royce Gruenler has. He points out that a person who makes a statement like the one in Luke 11:20 is implicitly speaking from a sense of his own identity. Jesus is here specifically intending "to exercise this unusual authority because he understands that he is acting as the mediating agent in realizing the powerful invasion of the reign of God. He is virtually claiming divine prerogatives. He is manifesting the power of God in a new exodus and is exhibiting that power in terms of his personal pronoun *I.*"[9] In other words, Jesus is taking himself to be much more than an ordinary human being.

Jesus the Unique

Taken alone, this one saying cannot carry the entire weight of the case against Jesus' being either a liar or a lunatic. But when it is added to other sayings that fit the criterion of dissimilarity, a strong case can be made. So what comes through the stringent test?

1. Jesus' assumption of authority. This is seen in both his exorcisms and his teaching style and language. Over and over, rather than deferring to or commenting on a text of Scripture, Jesus on his own authority boldly says, in Aramaic, "Amen, amen [truly, truly], *I* say to you," using the emphatic *I,* a grammatical nicety that is not so noticeable in English translations. This use of *amen* is "without parallel in the whole of Jewish literature and the rest of the New Testament."[10] In the Sermon on the Mount, itself a masterpiece unparalleled in literature, Jesus says six times, "You have heard it said . . ." Then he continues, "But I say to you . . ." (Matthew 5:21-47), thus putting his authority above that of previous teachers where they disagree with him.

2. *Jesus' reference to God as* abba, *an Aramaic word used by children to refer to their father.* There is no instance recorded in pre-Christian Palestinian Judaism that God was addressed as *abba* by Jews in prayer. That would be to say "Daddy" to the Master of the universe. The early church did do this, but as Martin Hengel says, "The only explanation of the significance of the Aramaic cry 'Abba' in Paul's Gentile-Christian communities is that it goes back to Jesus himself."[11] In his use of this term Jesus is enhancing the Jewish understanding of God, emphasizing the warmth of his filial relation to us, his children.[12]

3. *Jesus' teaching on the kingdom of God.* Two features deserve attention. First is the association of the kingdom of God with the presence of Jesus (Mark 1:14-15); the second is the association of the kingdom of God not just with Israel, the people of God, but also with individuals. When Jesus cast out a demon from an individual, the kingdom of God was present with "you," the people of God (Luke 11:20).[13] The theme of the kingdom of God fits the *criterion of multiple attestation* as well, because one finds it in every layer of tradition, including parables, proverbial statements and ethical teachings.

4. *Jesus' teaching by parables.* Though there are some two thousand rabbinic parables that New Testament scholars have been studying alongside those of Jesus, none of them (with the exception of seven found in the Old Testament) derive from either Jesus' own day or before. Jeremias says, "We find nothing to be compared with the parables of Jesus, whether in the entire intertestamental literature of Judaism, in the Essene writings, in Paul, or in Rabbinic literature [at least the Rabbinic literature during or before the time of Jesus]."[14] When later rabbis used parables, they did so to interpret Scripture. Jesus did not use them like this. Rather, as we have already seen, his

parables were means of calling the hearer to decision (see pages 119-21 and 125-29). Of the seven parables, the only true Old Testament parallel is the parable of the poor man and his lamb which Nathan told to David (2 Samuel 12:1-10).[15]

5. Jesus' teaching that the good news is for those on the margins of society. The marginalized of his day included the poor, tax collectors, sinners, prostitutes, social outcasts, the lame, the blind, the demonized, the uneducated, the ignorant, the oppressed, women and children. "The message that God wants to have dealings with sinners and only with sinners and that his love extends to them is without parallel at the time. It is unique."[16] We saw a glimpse of this in the Gospel sections examined in the previous chapter.

6. Jesus' actions in associating with (especially dining with) those on the margins of society. More even than today, table fellowship was a powerful expression of acceptance. One ate and dined only with members of one's own social class, and only within the bounds of the purity rules.[17] With seemingly deliberate intent, Jesus constantly broke those rules. It becomes obvious that the Gospels' multiple references to Jesus' dining are making a point. Jesus was saying by doing; he was demonstrating that the kingdom of God was not to be equated with the social stratification of ordinary Jewish society. In fact, Jesus more often seemed to be associating with the down and out and telling stories about banquets for outcasts (Luke 14:15-20) than dining with people like Simon (Luke 7:36-50) and Zacchaeus (Luke 19:1-10). This action and this message make Jesus unique.

7. Jesus' self-conscious association of himself with the Suffering Servant of Isaiah (especially Isaiah 53). This is sometimes challenged as an invention of the early church, but Jeremias makes a strong case for its historicity.[18] Certainly it fits the criterion of dissimilarity, for the Jews of Jesus' day were not looking for a suffering servant but a messiah, a powerful human being who was to be sent by God not just to restore Israel to its former glory, as in the time of King David, but to bring the state of Israel to political, social and cultural dominance among the nations.

I. Howard Marshall, after conducting a similar, though more thorough, analysis of Jesus' uniqueness, draws this conclusion:

> [Jesus] stands alone; he has no equals. It might be objected that this is precisely the picture of him that we might expect from the Christian tradition, but in fact we have built our case above purely on material that passes radical criteria for authenticity, and we have not used the vast amount of corroborative evidence that can be gleaned from the areas of tradition that could be said to stand under suspicion when radical tests are applied.[19]

When the *criterion of coherence* is applied, other passages of the Gospels come flooding back into relevance. The Gospels contain many accounts that don't meet the criterion of dissimilarity but do cohere with these passages. Indeed, the Gospels taken in their entirety present a coherent picture of a coherent person. The Jesus we see before his death is even coherent with the most amazing event of all: the resurrection.

Jesus the Man of His Time

The second way to both use skepticism and respond to it is to examine the social context in which Jesus is embedded. With the methods of the original Quest of the Historical Jesus well lost sight of, and the New Quest still producing some interesting if not accurate results, what has come to be called a Third Quest has been launched.[20] What it assumes is that Jesus would have to be a man of his time. So what was his time, and in light of his time how can we best understand the Jesus of the Gospels?

What emerges from these studies is a person whose concerns were the concerns of the people of his day. People beset by sickness and demonic possession needed to be healed; Jesus was one among a number of exorcists who cast out evil spirits. Israel was under the yoke of Rome—could that yoke be thrown off? In the meantime, how were people to live under Roman rule in light of the prophecy of the coming of a new Davidic king? Jesus responded with talk about the present and coming kingdom of God. The Pharisees called the people to a perfect keeping of the details of the Jewish law; the Essenes agreed but insisted that the true Israel had to withdraw completely from normal public life in a state ruled by Rome. What was true holiness, after all? The temple, the center of Jewish worship, was not the temple prophesied;[21] it had been built by Herod under the aegis of foreign rule. The priests were false priests. Where was the true temple?

The Third Quest focuses on these and other issues that were important to Jesus' contemporaries. It has helped us see with much more clarity Jesus as a man of his time.

One of the most recent entries into the field of Third Quest studies does make a strong case for a Jesus very like the one we saw in chapter nine. N. T. Wright has entered the arena in a major way with the first volume of a massive five-volume work.[22] It is too early to tell just how effective Wright will be in capturing the agreement of his fellow scholars, but it is clear that he already has their respect.[23]

In his first volume Wright examines in depth the self-understanding of the Jewish people in the decades before, during and somewhat after Jesus' life. He surveys the background history and social setting, the stories, symbols, practices and beliefs, and the future hope of Israel. Then he shows how Jesus both fit and didn't fit into this setting. Take his teaching about the kingdom of God:

> The strange thing about Jesus' announcement of the Kingdom of God was that he managed *both* to claim that he was fulfilling the old prophecies, the old hopes of Israel *and* to do so in a way which radically subverted them. The Kingdom of God is here, he seemed to be saying, *but it's not like you thought it was going to be.*[24]

Jesus also rejected the common ways that holiness was understood:

> Jesus was saying—in his actions as much as his words—that you didn't have to observe every last bit of the Torah before you would count as a real member of Israel. He was saying that you didn't have to make the journey to Jerusalem, offer sacrifice, and go through the purity rituals, in order to be regarded as clean, forgiven, and forgiven right here, where Jesus was, at this party, just by being there with him and welcoming his way of bringing in the

Kingdom. No wonder his family said he was out of his mind.[25]
In fact, Jesus saw himself as summing up in his own person the future of Israel. "He believed himself called to go out ahead of Israel, to meet the judgment in her place alone."[26] The current temple in Jerusalem would be destroyed in divine justice, but that was not the end of God's people or his presence in their midst. Jesus would replace the temple in function. He would redeem Israel. If Jesus thought of himself in these ways, then what is so odd about his going even further? Wright poses the question, "Why should such a person, a good first-century Jewish monotheist, not also come to hold the strange and risky belief that the one true God, the God of Israel, was somehow present and active in him and even *as* him?"[27]

Wright has used the methods employed in the Third Quest of the Historical Jesus. In so doing, he has shown that the picture of Jesus achieved through a traditional (though perhaps naive) reading may not be so far off the mark after all. A Third Quest Jesus will not, of course, emerge as a pious figure walking six inches above the ground. He will be a real, physical person living a normal human life. But in his humanity there will be clear signals of transcendence, more than casual hints that someone special has walked among us. Historical study of this sort goes a long way toward showing that it is rational to believe in a Jesus who in flesh and blood (not in some airy landscape of faith alone) thought of himself, if not as God, at least as standing in for God.

Face to Face Again with the Unexpected Jesus

In light of the above analysis, neither the fourth nor the fifth reason for skepticism—that the writers couldn't remember well enough to be accurate or that they invented a Jesus who privileged them as leaders—can be maintained. It is Jesus, not his followers, who is surprising and unique. His followers are depicted as misunderstanding him and his teaching, abandoning him when it might cost their lives, even betraying him. Surely this is not the picture early-church leaders would paint if it were not true.

Perhaps the most telling reason for rejecting the notion that the early church invented a Jesus of convenience—one who justified them in their lifestyle and belief, one who gave them authority to continue in power—is that the Jesus of the Gospels does none of these things. It is impossible for any Christian believer, whether in leadership or not, to read the Gospels and not feel challenged and humbled. No reader measures up to the stature of Christ; no one can contemplate the Sermon on the Mount and not feel weighed and found wanting. Leaders who claim authority from the New Testament had better be ready to live as the New Testament calls us to live.

The precise way that we approach the task of checking the reliability of the historical record ends up not being all that significant. In the words of Craig Blomberg,

> Whichever perspective is adopted at the outset, then, an identical conclusion may be reached. Whether by giving the gospels the benefit of the doubt which all narratives of purportedly historical events merit or by approaching them with an initial suspicion in which every detail must satisfy the criteria of authenticity, the verdict should remain the same. The gospels may be accepted as trustworthy accounts of what Jesus did and said.[28]

We are face to face with a historic person who makes demands on us far down into the reaches of his future.

The problem for the early church and us is not that the Gospels give us an untrustworthy picture of Jesus, but that they give us a picture that either brings us to our knees or sends us sadly away, knowing we should believe and follow Jesus but unwilling to do so.

So we must return to the argument of the previous chapter. Even by using highly skeptical methods of checking for historicity, we still get a picture of Jesus that brings us face to face with the dilemma: Is he who he thought he was, or is he a liar or a lunatic? We cannot maintain that he was a legend. There are too many reasons to think otherwise. How we respond to the dilemma is up to us.

The key to Christianity is the resurrection of Jesus Christ from the grave. That is the heart of the matter. For Christianity does not claim that Jesus was a good teacher and a fine man. It maintains that in Jesus, God broke into our world. His whole life was a demonstration of what God is like. And when men crucified him through envy and hatred on the first Good Friday, God raised him from the dead on Easter day, vindicating his claims, his teaching, his life and his sacrificial death.

That is, and always has been, the Christian claim. So if you want to examine the truth of Christianity, and whether or not you can credit the answers it gives to the problems of our world, it is to the resurrection you should turn.

MICHAEL GREEN, *THE DAY DEATH DIED*

————

The
Resurrection
of Jesus
11

M any Christians presenting the case for Christianity begin with
the subject of this chapter. To them it may seem odd that I have
delayed so long in getting to what they consider the heart
of the apologetic argument—the bodily resurrection of Jesus Christ.
Theologian J. I. Packer puts the point strongly:

The Easter event . . . demonstrated Jesus' deity; validated his teaching; attested the completion of his work of atonement for sin;
confirms his present cosmic dominion and his coming reappear-
ance as Judge; assures us that his personal pardon, presence, and
power in people's lives today is fact; and guarantees each believer's
own reembodiment by resurrection in the world to come.[1]

If the resurrection can prove all that, then it should be at the top of
the list of reasons for accepting Christianity as true. And it is.

The problem is that from a modern scientific point of view the
resurrection is incredible. To prove one complex, doubtful matter
(Christianity) by another simpler but even more fantastic matter (the

resurrection) is foolhardy. Or so would say many modern people indisposed to believe either, especially if it would cause them to radically reorient their lives, as belief in either one most reasonably will do.

This difficulty does not, of course, remove the value of an apologetic based on the resurrection—not if the argument for the resurrection can be shown to be strong, not if the resurrection is the best explanation for the evidence we have. As we saw in chapter seven, the case for miracles must deal with the evidence for miracles. And that is the goal of this chapter.

The strength of the argument usually given for the resurrection, however, can itself be increased when it is seen in light of the evidence for the character of Jesus. If anyone were ever to be raised from the dead, it would be a person like Jesus. If he could cast out demons with such success, heal the lame, give sight to the blind, baffle the religious experts with his theological wisdom, reorient the lives of prostitutes, tax collectors, and Pharisees, and live a life with which no one could honestly find fault, then the notion of his resurrection is not so far-fetched.

For a long time it has been my fascination with Jesus—his character, the brilliance and wisdom of his teaching, the depth of his compassion, the endlessness of his grace in forgiving sin—that has kept me in the faith. "To whom shall we go?" Peter once asked. "You have the words of eternal life. We believe and know that you are the Holy One of God" (John 6:68-69). Still, as is clear from the Gospels of Mark and Luke, it took the resurrection to convince Peter and the other disciples that Jesus was Lord of lords and King of kings, worthy of being followed without reservation. Though Jesus is fascinating as a person, it is the resurrection that confirms the ground for that fascination.

The Importance of the Resurrection
What if the resurrection did not occur? What effect would it have on the nature and character of Christianity? What would it do to my faith and the faith of millions around the world?

First and most important, the authority for Jesus' claim to forgive sins would be utterly undermined. If he couldn't forgive sins, then not only was he deluded about himself, but he was selling a fake salvation. He was then anything but a good man. But if Jesus did, as he promised, "give his life a ransom for many" (Mark 10:45) and rise from the dead three days later, we have solid ground for our trust in him. We know why he could say "Your sins are forgiven" (Mark 2:5).

Second, if Jesus did not rise from the dead, the distinctives of his ethical teaching are not worth following. Of course, Jesus said many things other great teachers have said. But Jesus also called for profound sacrifice and seemingly foolish action. Take his commands in the Sermon on the Mount (Matthew 5—7) about turning the other cheek, his equation of lust with adultery and his advice to take no thought for the physical needs of the future. Why should I feel guilty when I lust? Why not relax and enjoy it? Why should we believe him when he called blessed those who mourn, those who are meek, those who are persecuted for righteousness' sake? These teachings are beyond reasonable ethics; they demand a transcendent foundation.

Third, there would be little foundation for hope for any of us for a life beyond the grave. To be sure, many Jews in Jesus' day believed in a general resurrection of the dead. They trusted the teaching of the Old Testament prophets and the rabbis. Many today, however, are outside the Jewish tradition and would have little reason to gain confidence from those sources. If Jesus did rise from the dead, of course, all people can have hope. All can follow the apostle Paul in seeing Jesus as the "firstfruits of those who have fallen asleep" (1 Corinthians 15:20).

Paul, as we have seen in chapter seven (pages 99-102), makes a great deal of the importance of the resurrection for just the reasons I have been noting here: "If Christ has not been raised, our preaching is useless and so is your faith. . . . You are still in your sins" (1 Corinthians 15:14, 17).

Did the resurrection really happen? What is the evidence? Is it rational to believe in the resurrection? What is the "best explanation" of the data we have?

The Rationality of the Resurrection

The resurrection has been the subject of such intensive study that I will not try to add anything to what others have said. Nor will I go into exhaustive detail. For that I suggest you consult one of the book-length treatises listed in the bibliography. Basically, there are seven reasons to believe that Jesus was raised from the dead. We will look at each in turn.

First, the disciples and early followers of Jesus believed that Jesus was resurrected. For this we have the evidence not only of the Gospel stories but also of the accounts in Acts (a history of the early church, the fifth book of the New Testament) of Peter's, Stephen's and Paul's preaching (Acts 2:32; 3:14; 17:18, 31-32). Then too there are the letters of Paul and other apostles, which are replete with allusions to the resurrected Christ (Romans 1:4; 6:5; Philippians 3:10; Hebrews 6:2—to name a few). If the early leaders in the Christian movement had not actually believed that Jesus was raised and now alive with God, they would themselves have been selling a salvation they knew was fake. For this there would have been no reason, for over and over again they were persecuted for their preaching. The agony of their beatings would have ended if they had simply said, "Sorry. Just kidding. I made it all up." Instead, holding their ground, they died for their faith.

Blaise Pascal saw this long ago:

The hypothesis that the Apostles were knaves is quite absurd. Follow it out to the end and imagine these twelve men meeting after Jesus's death and conspiring to say that he had risen from the dead. This means attacking all the powers that be. The human heart is singularly susceptible to fickleness, to change, to promises, to bribery. One of them had only to deny his story under these inducements, or still more because of possible imprisonment, tortures and death, and they would all have been lost.[2]

Assessing this evidence for the belief of the disciples, even Michael Grant, a historian who does not believe the resurrection took place, concludes that the early followers of Jesus were "utterly convinced" that Jesus had been resurrected.[3]

Second, the tomb was empty. All four Gospels mention this detail (Matthew 28:1-10; Mark 16:8; Luke 24:1-11; John 20:1-10). On what is now called Easter morning, several women went to the tomb to anoint Jesus' body. They found the grave—a cave that had been sealed with a large stone—open and empty. One of the women, Mary, told the apostles, and Peter and John were the first to investigate. Inside they found the graveclothes, lying as if the body they had held had simply passed through them.

Michael Grant, doubtful of much else, nonetheless yields the evidence of the open tomb:

> Even if the historian chooses to regard the youthful apparition as extra-historical, he cannot justifiably deny the empty tomb. True, this discovery, as so often, is described differently by the various Gospels—as critical pagans early pointed out. But if we apply the same sort of evidence that we would apply to any other ancient literary sources, then the evidence is firm and plausible enough to necessitate the conclusion that the tomb was indeed found empty.[4]

Mark, of course, does not call the "young man dressed in a white robe" (Mark 16:4) an *apparition* (that is the interpretative language of a modern historian), but while Grant doubts the reality of the youth, he still acknowledges that evidence for the empty tomb is more than sufficient to establish it as a fact.

The significance of the empty tomb is, of course, that the body of Jesus was missing. This was a bodily resurrection. It was not that his spirit or soul took on the appearance of a body. Though that postresurrection body was to some extent different from his precrucifixion body (it could also pass through walls), it was in all important ways the same body (it had the scars of his crucifixion and could handle food). It was indeed Jesus who was raised from the dead, not another person in his place pretending to be him, nor a mere ghost.

Nonetheless, the empty tomb did not in itself produce belief in the resurrection. Rather, the initial assumption was that someone had removed the body—stolen it or reburied it (John 20:2). What convinced the disciples were the multiple appearances Jesus made in his postresurrection body.

Third is the testimony of women. The importance of one detail may be lost on us today. That is the fact that women are credited both with the discovery that the grave was empty and with the first postresurrection encounters with Jesus. In Jesus' day the testimony of women was not even allowed in court. "If the reports of the empty tomb were invented, it is difficult to understand why their inventors should have embellished their accounts of the 'discovery' with something virtually guaranteed to discredit them."[5] That women were the first witnesses must be true; there would be no other reason for including the detail.

Fourth are the many accounts in the New Testament of Jesus' appearance after the crucifixion. Matthew, Luke, John and Acts all contain vivid records (Matthew 28:8-10; Luke 24:13-43; John 20:11-29; Acts 1:1-11). A summary of them is a major part of one of the earliest descriptions of what the first Christians believed. Paul, in a letter to the church at Corinth in the early 50s A.D., wrote:

> Now, brothers, I want to remind you of the gospel I preached to you, which you received and on which you have taken your stand. By this gospel you are saved, if you hold firmly to the word I preached to you. Otherwise you have believed in vain.
>
> For what I received I passed on to you as of first importance: that Christ died for our sins according to the Scriptures, that he was buried, that he was raised on the third day according to the Scriptures, and that he appeared to Peter, and then to the Twelve. After that, he appeared to more than five hundred of the brothers at the same time, most of whom are still living, though some have fallen asleep. Then he appeared to James, then to all the apostles, and last of all he appeared to me also, as to one abnormally born. (1 Corinthians 15:1-8)

For our purposes, this "creed" is especially significant for its date. It occurs in a letter written in the early 50s but it dates to a very few years after Jesus' death. Gary Habermas explains how we can be sure of the early source of this list of resurrection appearances:

That this material is traditional and pre-Pauline is evident from the technical terms *delivered* and *received,* the parallelism and somewhat stylized content, the proper names of Cephas and James, the non-Pauline words, and the possibility of an Aramaic original.

Concerning the date of this creed, critical scholars almost always agree that it has an early origin, usually placing it in the A.D. 30s. Paul most likely received this material during his first visit in Jerusalem with Peter and James, who are included in the list of appearances (1 Cor 15:5, 7). In fact, Fuller, Hunter, and Pannenberg are examples of critical scholars who date Paul's receiving of this creed from three to eight years after the Crucifixion itself. And if Paul received it at such an early date, the creed itself would be even earlier because it would have existed before the time he was told. And the facts upon which the creed was originally based would be earlier still. We are for all practical purposes back to the original events.[6]

The implications of the early date are sometimes missed: first, that these "traditions" about Jesus are "unlikely to have been distorted because the period [after the events occurred] was so brief"; and second, that "it would be incredible if such traditions did not reflect the mind of the Master who had been so recently with the disciples."[7]

In the Gospels the stories of the appearances bear all manner of the marks of eyewitness accounts. Take one of these accounts, in John 20:[8]

Early on the first day of the week, while it was still dark, Mary of Magdala went to the tomb and saw that the stone had been removed from the entrance. So she came running to Simon Peter and the other disciple, the one whom Jesus loved, and said, "They have taken the Lord out of the tomb, and we don't know where they have put him!"

So Peter and the other disciple started for the tomb. Both were running, but the other disciple outran Peter and reached the tomb first. He bent over and looked in at the strips of linen lying there but did not go in. Then Simon Peter, who was behind him, arrived and went into the tomb. He saw the strips of linen lying there, as well as the burial cloth that had been around Jesus' head. The cloth was folded up by itself, separate from the linen. Finally the other disciple, who had reached the tomb first, also went inside. He saw and believed. (They still did not understand from Scripture that Jesus had to rise from the dead.)

Notice the detail. Mary saw that the tomb was empty, but that just led her to believe that someone had taken the body. She did not just leap to belief across her ordinary incredulity regarding supernatural events. It took more than an empty tomb to convince even this woman, one who in Jesus' day would have been considered improperly credulous.

Peter and John "run" to the tomb, and one—probably the younger John (usually identified as "the disciple Jesus loved")—arrives first. He is reticent to enter. But the bold Peter whom we meet in every Gospel runs right in. There is a consistency between the events and the persons involved in them.

The graveclothes are lying in a very specific but peculiar fashion, again a sign of authenticity.

Finally, John "believes," but we are not told what or how much. Some scholars hold that he concluded that Jesus had risen from the dead because no grave robber would stop to take off the graveclothes before stealing the body.[9] In any case, John believed somewhat less than he would eventually believe when he and the other followers of Jesus saw what the Scriptures had prophesied. The Gospels avoid showing the disciples as more than ordinary people trying to understand what has happened but not yet fully apprised.

Fifth, the disciples were transformed from puzzled and frightened people to confident, bold proclaimers of the good news. After the resurrection, the disciples learned from the teachings of the resurrected Lord. In the ascension, some forty days after the resurrection, Jesus left them, having commissioned them to spread the good news first in Israel and then throughout the world. On the day of Pentecost, a short time after the ascension, the followers of Jesus in Jerusalem were filled with the

Holy Spirit and spoke in foreign languages. Challenged that they were all drunk, Peter boldly proclaimed the resurrection of Jesus and explained what had happened. After that the small, cowering band of followers immediately became a community of faith, headed by tough, tenacious apostles who boldly preached the gospel of Christ publicly and privately. The story is told in the Acts of the Apostles and is reflected in the letters of Paul, James, John and the writer of Hebrews.

What explains this radical transformation? The New Testament attributes it to the work of the Holy Spirit, directly connected to the redemptive work of Jesus. The disciples believed that their Lord and Savior had lived among them, died and been resurrected. They believed that they were commissioned to spread the good news throughout the world, beginning where they were. The gospel did indeed spread amazingly rapidly from Israel to the rest of the Middle East around the Mediterranean to Asia Minor, Greece and Rome. Even today the spread continues as some missionaries risk life and limb to bring the message of Jesus to the violent streets of the world's inner cities and the deep forests of South America and Papua New Guinea, while others risk ridicule and ostracism to make Christ understood on the campuses of secular universities.

Tenacity of belief does not, of course, prove the truth of the things believed. Many people have given their lives for a lie. But there should be an explanation for the radical transformation of character of the followers of Jesus. They were ordinary people from the center of ordinary Jewish society. They were not a band of rabble-rousers, used to the hurly-burly of street fighting. They became bold challengers of the status quo only because they clearly believed that Jesus had come back from the dead, that he had somehow effected the redemption of Israel and all in the world who would believe and follow him. They would never have become preachers of such a message without believing that the resurrection really occurred. They would never have been transformed if the very power of God were not at work.

Sixth, Jesus became understood in highly exalted terms immediately after the resurrection. The Synoptic Gospels depict the disciples as only gradually coming to understand who Jesus is, and at the end of his life they mostly get it wrong. They abandon Jesus as he is tried, sentenced and crucified. They cower together in secret, not abandoning each other but reluctant to be known as his followers. And well they might, because they would themselves be subject to some of the charges that put Jesus on the cross. The resurrection was the event that changed everything—made all of Jesus' teachings about God, about them and about himself fall in line.

Over and over, Jesus had referred to himself as *Son of Man.* Readers not acquainted with the Old Testament think this title is simply a phrase used by Jesus to indicate his solidarity with humanity. It is instead, as an allusion to the *son of man* in Daniel 7, and thus a veiled claim to a very exalted status.[10] Of course, it is obvious from the opening words of the Gospel of Mark—"the beginning of the gospel about Jesus Christ, the Son of God" (1:1)—and the comment by the centurion watching Jesus die on the cross—"Surely this man was the Son of God!" (15:39)—that Mark has a very high view of Jesus. In any case, very early on the emerging community of faith began referring to Jesus in words suggesting deity. As Alister McGrath says,

> Jesus was not venerated as a dead prophet or rabbi . . . he was worshipped as the living and risen Lord.
>
> At several points in the New Testament, words originally referring to God himself are applied to Jesus. . . . In Romans 10:13 [A.D. 57] Paul states that "everyone who calls upon the name of the Lord [Jesus in this case] will be saved"—yet the original of the Old Testament quotation (Joel 2:32) is actually a statement to the effect that everyone who calls upon the name of *God* will be saved.
>
> In Philippians 2:10 Paul alters an Old Testament prophecy to the effect that everyone will one day bow at the name of God (Isaiah 45:23) to refer to Jesus.[11]

Where did this high Christology come from if not from the apostles' grasp of what Jesus had been showing them before the crucifixion? We are not given direct information on the specific teaching Jesus gave his disciples in his postresurrection appearances. But surely such a high Christology could have been part of it. In any case, the so-called high Christology of the Gospel of John, in which Jesus is depicted as fully and openly conscious of his divine nature (for example, John 8:58; 10:34-38) is grounded in the historical reality we see reflected in the Synoptic Gospels, which were written, presumably, a decade or two before.

There are three more reasons for concluding that the earliest church believed in the historicity of the resurrection: (1) the fact that baptism and the Lord's Supper demand a view of Jesus as resurrected, (2) the experience of Christians from the first century and down through the ages that Jesus is the present risen Lord and (3) a final, telling one that I will deal with in detail. Before considering this seventh reason, however, we should consider the alternative explanations that have been given for the data I have been using to argue the case.

Alternate Explanations of the Data

First, the disciples stole the body. This is the oldest alternative theory, having been proposed by the religious leaders of Jesus' day. They paid the soldiers guarding the tomb to say that the disciples had whisked the body away (Matthew 28:11-15).

But there are a number of reasons that this is not likely. (1) The graveclothes were not disturbed; they suggest that the body had come through them in the way a butterfly emerges from a cocoon, not that the body had been stolen and the graveclothes removed. (2) The disciples had no reason to steal the body; they did not believe that Jesus was going to be raised from the dead. (3) The disciples were too frightened to challenge a guard. (4) The guards, if sleeping, would have awakened at the noise of a stone rolling away; besides, if they could have identified the disciples as the thieves, they would not have been asleep. (5) The disciples would not later have died under persecution just to maintain a fiction of Jesus' resurrection; they would not have tried to offer a salvation they knew was fake. (6) A plot to steal the body and perpetrate a resurrection hoax would have unraveled as did the Watergate conspiracy.

Second, Jesus swooned or fainted on the cross, revived in the tomb and then wandered off somewhere unknown. This is not credible because (1) special care was taken to see that he was dead; (2) the blood and water that came from the wound in his side (John 19:34) indicated that he had died; (3) Jesus had been so brutalized that he wouldn't have had the strength to move the stone that covered the opening of the grave; and (4) the noise of the rolling stone would have wakened the guard.

Third, the disciples who saw Jesus after the resurrection were "victims of hysterical delusions."[12] (1) There are too many reported appearances under too many different conditions for this explanation to be tenable. (2) There was no expectation of his return from the dead. (3) "Only certain kinds of people, such as the highly imaginative, suffer from hallucinations."[13]

The Final Telling Reason

If my sense of the power of an argument is to be trusted, I think that there is a one more telling reason for believing that the resurrection of Jesus really occurred.

Seventh, there is a continuity and coherence between the resurrection and the entirety of Jesus' life. Jesus was always doing the unexpected. But the unexpected always turned out to make great sense. Think of the matters we have already noted in chapters eight and nine above:

☐ He forgave sins instead of immediately healing the paralytic.
☐ He ate with tax collectors, outcasts, sinners.
☐ He touched lepers and healed them.
☐ He accepted children as important.
☐ He used a hated Samaritan as a good example.
☐ He spoke with authority, not like the rabbis.
☐ He treated women on a par with men.
☐ He told parables of a unique type, stories that cut to the heart of his listeners.
☐ He prayed to God on intimate terms *(Abba).*

☐ He pointed to himself as the one who had come from God to bring salvation to people.

☐ He said that in him the kingdom of God was present.

☐ After the resurrection, the disciples realized that he had predicted his death and resurrection and that they had not understood him.

In short, Jesus did the unexpected, but he was not bizarre. What he did was credible after the fact, even though without a better understanding of the Old Testament than characterized Jesus' contemporaries it could not have been predicted.[14] His actions fit with his character. So this final reason for believing that the resurrection really did take place is the sense it makes of all of his life.

If we are looking for a "best explanation," as explained in chapter six, then here, I would say, we have really found one. Given the evidence of Jesus' character and the concrete evidence of the disciples' belief, the empty tomb, the postcrucifixion appearances to the disciples, the transformation of their character, and the failure of counterexplanations to account for the data, the best explanation is that the bodily resurrection of Jesus really occurred. It is, indeed, just the sort of thing that Jesus—given who he showed us he was during his life—would do if indeed he were the Son of God.

In recent years there has been a noticeable increase in the number of intellectuals who embrace historic Christianity as a rational worldview. In philosophy, at least seven journals are produced by Christian theists and in 1978 the Society of Christian Philosophers was formed. This society includes several hundred professionally trained philosophers who embrace some form of the Christian faith. . . . Taken by themselves, the trends listed do not prove Christianity is true or even rational. But these trends do point to the fact that a number of thinkers believe that secularism is an inadequate view of the world and that a rational apologetic can be given for historic Christianity.

J. P. MORELAND, *SCALING THE SECULAR CITY*

———

The
Rationality
of Christian
Faith
12

T he third reason for believing that Christianity is true is that the
Christian worldview deals consistently and coherently with the
data of experience and gives the "best explanation" of the tough
issues that trouble us.

In principle, this reason claims to include all of human experience:
personal experience, the records of history and biography, the data
and theories of all the sciences. It claims that in the final analysis all
of reality is best explained by the tenets of Christianity and their
implications. It claims that Christianity provides the most convincing
framework in which to address, for example, the question of human
nature, the nature of the human psyche, the structure of DNA, the
behavior of every animal from the gnat to the gnu and every person
from East to West. The claim is not that the details of any one of these
are a direct readout of the Bible or Christian theology, but that what
we discover by every variety of reflection and scholarship is best understood when placed in the context of Christian thought.

It is obvious, therefore, that in this chapter we can only scratch the surface of this reason for believing Christianity, only glimpse a sliver of the great shaft of light we could see by looking longer and harder at more issues than I can cover here.

I will, in fact, deal only with one issue—one of the most vital issues we have to face, I believe, especially in a world where the many nations, cultures and subcultures disagree so vastly with each other. The issue is ethics: How can we as human beings tell the difference between right and wrong? On what foundation are moral decisions based? This issue in itself is vast and worthy of several books on its own.[1] So what follows here is more illustrative than exhaustive.

A Foundation for Ethical Decisions

One of the matters close to the essence of human nature is our propensity for making moral judgments. Regardless of our background, our society, our culture, whether we are highly sophisticated in our moral ruminations or simply act naively, we constantly judge actions to be right, wrong or some combination of the two. The problem for people in the twentieth century is whether there is any foundation for the judgments we make. If or when—and often it's *when*—we are challenged about the judgments we have made, what basis will we use to justify our judgments? Is there any?

James Q. Wilson opens his essay "What Is Moral, and How Do We Know It?" with an excellent summary of the current situation:

Almost every important tendency in modern thought has questioned the possibility of making moral judgments. Analytical philosophy asserts that moral statements are expressions of emotion lacking any rational or scientific basis. Marxism derides morality and religion as "phantoms formed in the human brain," "ideological reflexes" that are, at best, mere sublimates of material circumstances. Nietzsche writes dismissively that morality is but the herd instinct of the individual. Existentialists argue that man must choose his values without having any sure compass by which to guide those choices. Cultural anthropology as practiced by many of its most renowned scholars claims that amid the exotic diversity of human life there can be found no universal laws of right conduct. . . . All of science seems the enemy of moral confidence, because its method requires that we separate factual statements that can be verified from "value" statements, which cannot.[2]

Although Wilson lists a panorama of perspectives—analytic philosophy, Marxism, Nietzsche, existentialism, cultural anthropology—all of them have one element in common. They assume a naturalistic world—a universe where God is dead (or, better, never was alive). Wilson doesn't put it this way, but the real problem in such a world is whether we can be good without God.[3] Is there any way to have a rational foundation for our moral motions?

We must note carefully exactly what the issue is. The question is not whether people distinguish between right and wrong. Everyone except, perhaps, a very few psychopaths does that. Even the proverbial superskeptical student, fresh from reflecting on Nietzsche, who says, "I am a nihilist. I don't believe there is a difference between right and wrong," will be furious if the teacher assigns a very low grade to a paper the student thinks deserves a better mark. Among students fairness is a universal norm, and they demand that their teachers practice it—at least when it comes to judging their work.

Moreover, the issue is *not* the specific content of the morality. In fact, there is at least some general conformity in what people judge to be wrong. That murder is wrong is about as universal a norm as one can find among all peoples (even though some groups may not use that term for killing a person outside their tribe or their tight-knit social group). Love is generally commended, even if it does not extend to the obligation to love one's enemy as it does with Jesus (Matthew 5:44). Care for children is also virtually universal.[4]

Rather, the issue is whether there is any actual reason that these norms are norms. Why should hatred and murder be wrong and love and tender care be right? Wilson, as we have seen above, lists at least some of the reasons this question has been so hard to answer. Modern atheistic philosophy has reduced ethics to emotion, ideology, herd instinct and human choice. Without a moral realm distinct from the realm of brute fact, everything is just fact. The values people adhere to are only as authoritative as those who claim the values. Ethical relativism is, to be sure, the natural consequence of naturalism.

Getting *Ought* from *Is*

Let's look more closely at why that is so. If all there is is matter and what it does, then all there is is *is*. There can be no *ought*.

Let's be more concrete. For example, in human action what *is?* Tender care for children is; child abuse is. Love and respect between persons are; hatred and fury are. Defense of the helpless is; violence and rape are. There is no need to go on. The world of human action is filled with both the commendable and the despicable. That is, we think that some actions are commendable and others despicable. And we have no trouble acting as if the commendable is right and the despicable wrong. But are they really?

How can these actions actually be right or wrong? Only if there is a difference between *is* and *ought*. But how can there be a difference between *is* and *ought* in a world that just is? The distinction is impossible to make on rational grounds.

If there is to be such a difference, it will have to be because some things in the world do not conform to something outside the world by which they are measured. There will have to be an existent moral realm or, better, an existent personal Being who in and of himself stands as the repository of goodness. Otherwise, we are left only with such options as Wilson lists. The words *commendable* and *despicable*, *right* and *wrong*, become only labels for emotional reactions (what any *I* commends or despises) or terms hiding suppressed desires (what any *I* is deluded into thinking it has chosen) or yearnings for personal power (what any *I* wants or doesn't want) or the choice (agonized or flippant, thoughtful or brash) of each *I* who by its own will creates the good by deciding or acting or both.

Wilson rejects both the view that God's character of goodness stands behind the genuine distinction between right and wrong and the despair of the philosophers he lists in his first paragraph. He calls for a return to the notion of a universal human character, not in order to identify some rules universal to all people in all cultures (this, he says, has been tried and found impossible) but in order to identify universal human affections leading to a variety of similar yet somewhat diverse moral rules and ethical decisions. Specifically, he notes the "sense of empathy and fairness" that emerges as a result of "universal attachment between child and parent"; these "moral senses" are "to some important degree innate and . . . appear spontaneously amid the routine intimacies of family life."[5] Wilson then goes on to show how this origin of moral motions develops in practice and extends to various family relations and out into the business world. He is not naive about how these moral motions are sidetracked into immorality or confronted by paradox, as when the affection between members of a family or a clan develops into exclusion of other human beings from the benefits of social order. Nor is he sanguine about the character of these common human affections:

> We may disagree about what is natural, but we cannot escape the fact that we have a nature—that is, a set of traits and predispositions that set limits to what we must do. That nature is mixed: we fear violent death but sometimes deliberately risk it; we want to improve our own happiness but sometimes work for the happiness of others; we value our individuality but are tormented by the prospect of being alone.[6]

Oddly, Wilson does not seem to notice that the very goal he is trying to achieve—securing a foundation for the distinction between right and wrong—is belied by two things.

First is his own acknowledgment of the duplicity of the human character. "Human nature cannot be described by any single disposition," he says, and then calls us to work with "several moral principles" based on our several "dispositions." "Prudent action" involves "striking a delicate balance among [our moral senses] and between them and prudent self interest."[7] This I take to be a counsel of despair. Which of my moral motions are right? Which wrong? How do

I begin to know how to "strike a delicate balance" between conflicting claims?

Second, Wilson has not even begun to distinguish between *is* and *ought*. He remains in the realm of *is*. Of course, he has told us what I too take to be true—to wit, that we have a character. But he has not told us how we know which aspects of our character—which affections—we *ought* to act on and which we *ought* to suppress. Nor has he told us how we can identify what balance might just be an *is* and what balance is really an *ought*.

In short, Wilson has not moved us a half-inch from the position of those philosophers he rejects in the first paragraph of his essay. What he said there is still true: among modern thinkers accepting the absence of God, so far no one has found a basis on which to distinguish between right and wrong. I maintain that it is in principle impossible for one ever to be found. If we are to be good (really good, not just thought to be good), a God who is good will have to exist.

The Issue Reconsidered

Perhaps I have been too hasty in concluding that God is necessary for morality. So let's raise the issue in a different way by asking, Why should moral motions require a foundation? Why don't we just observe that morality is a fact about us and then try to learn how to adjudicate our disagreements, if not rationally, at least peaceably?

There are at least three reasons this is not satisfactory. The first is an obvious practical reason. What if our disagreements are so vast and all-encompassing that one of us thinks it's quite moral to kill the other? This happens all the time, especially with people groups who wish to do so-called ethnic cleansing. Such disagreements are not going to be settled peaceably.

Second, why should peace itself be accepted as a major value? Is not valor at arms also a virtue? How can valor be expressed without conflict? The very content of our ethical norms may be such that resolution of conflict cannot be done peaceably.

Third, the fact of our moral judgments does not itself ground them.

Let's say that everyone believes that the world is flat (many people did at one time). That does not make it flat. The belief that the world is flat is a fact about what we believe, not a justification for our belief. That everyone shares the belief just means that no one is going to ask us to justify it. But when the evidence comes in that the world is really round, we will have to question our belief. Let's say someone sets out to sail west from Spain and without turning around ends up back in Spain. That anomaly cries out for explanation. Flatlanders will have a difficult time handling that datum.

The only way we can argue that some action is right (say, loving our children) and another action is wrong (say, beating our children) is if there really is a realm of goodness where the terms *right* and *wrong* get their definitive character.[8] Let's use that word so rejected by our own culture, the word *absolute*. If there is no absolute good, there can be no more than opinion. There needs to be a category in which *right* and *wrong* have an existence other than the one we give them by using the words. That is, the distinction to which the words *right* and *wrong* point has to actually exist. Without this, *right* and *wrong* are simply opinions we hold, having no more validity than the fact that we hold them.

This, of course, is simply a repeat of the argument given above. If there is no moral value to facticity (and in a totally natural world of matter and energy, there *is* no moral value to facticity), then we cannot derive value from fact.[9]

An Argument from Evolution

For the sake of argument and our attempt to understand the options, let's assume what naturally follows from naturalism—to wit, that we have evolved from nonliving matter. Whatever we are we are by processes of ordinary nature and not by being created by a God or gods. Morality is a result of the evolutionary process; it has survival value. From this standpoint, our insistence on acting as if there were a real difference between right and wrong is a fact about us that needs no further explanation. We are what we are, people who insist on acting with moral motions—no reason for it—just a matter of fact.

At first this may look like a reasonable explanation. After all, beings who develop attitudes of benevolence toward their fellow beings are more likely to survive to produce other beings like them than are those who wreak havoc on their kind.[10]

But we must realize that what has been explained here is only the fact of our morality, just the fact that we have developed moral motions. It does not give us a ground for these motions. It means as well that this fact of our insistence on acting and judging our and others' actions within a moral compass is an illusion. We commonly assume that our moral motions are based on something real, but they are not. They are very, very useful fictions, but fictions nonetheless.

In this case, the discovery that there is no foundation for our distinctions between right and wrong may well be counterevolutionary. That is, coming to believe what we now take to be the truth—that our morality is just opinion—may well prompt us to be less self-disciplined. Surely on the evening news we have occasionally seen people, some of them quite young, who have lost a binding sense of right and wrong and have lashed out with such antisocial behavior as violence, rape and murder. A world in which continued existence of the human race is predicated on everyone's believing what is not true is a sad world indeed.

Bad news is, of course, sometimes true and ought not be rejected because it is bad. But some bad news is simply false—or, as some have put it, too bad to be true. If there is a genuine justification for believing that a transcendent realm of goodness actually exists, then it surely should be given a very close look. That is what Christianity provides.

A nihilistic and relativistic spirit has been growing throughout the twentieth century. I am not concerned that the failure of naturalistic explanations for morality will lead us en masse to start living as if there were no distinction between right and wrong. The moral sense is too ingrained in us for that. But it is not so ingrained in us that we— or many of us at least—will not do severe damage to each other and to our whole culture. Amid the moral confusion of our day, we desperately need to find agreement on basic moral issues. We will never do so if we come to believe that all we have are opinions grounded only in our emotions, our affections, our individual choices or our unconscious drives to power. I do not think our "survival" as a species is at stake, but our "survival" as a civilized society is.

A Christian Approach to Ethics

Any Christian approach to ethics begins from the presupposition that an infinite-personal and good God exists and that he has intentionally created the entire universe with us in it and has made himself known to us.

Skeptics may reasonably respond with incredulity, "To start with this presupposition is to start with a massive leap of faith. You are simply believing what you are trying to prove." Yes and no, I would retort.

Yes, this is a presupposition, but not necessarily an act of faith. It might be—and is for Christians—but it can be identified consciously (by Christians and anyone else) and examined for its truth by analyzing whether it actually serves to explain what we experience. For example, we experience a world that seems to us to exist apart from us. The idea that we create the world of our experience by our own powers of projection—that we are God, so to speak—does not seem correct to most of us, at least not to those we consider rational. Does the presupposition of the existence of a good and infinite-personal God explain why we perceive the world this way? Of course it does. Is it the only explanation? Perhaps not, but it is a reasonable one, especially if it should turn out that the presupposition offers insight into (even perhaps gives the "best explanation" of) the whys and wherefores of countless other of our experiences—such as love, knowledge, our compassion for others, our longing for a life that continues beyond the grave, even our abilities in science and technology.

In this chapter I will focus on the presupposition of the existence of God to see if it explains our experience of morality. Can it do what naturalism cannot do?

Indeed it can. If a good God exists and if he has intentionally brought the world into existence separate from him (that is, created it rather than emanating it), then the good for our world consists in its being what God intended it to be.[11] There is a transcendent realm, an absolute standard, on which the distinction between right and wrong is founded. What is right is what God wants; what is wrong is what he does not want. This is not because anything any kind of god might want is right (for some gods might not be good). It is because the God who actually exists is himself good. His character is coterminous with what goodness is.[12] Goodness for us, then, is being and doing what God wants us to be and do.

Christianity likewise proclaims that God created human beings in a special way; he made them in his own image (Genesis 1:26-27). Because of this, human beings bear similarities to God that no other of God's creatures does. Human beings have self-awareness, self-determination, the ability to know many but not all things, the ability to be creative and—for our purposes the most important—the ability to distinguish between right and wrong. Our moral capacity reflects the nature of God. Moreover, God has not left us to figure out what the good is simply on the basis of our innate moral nature. He has had personal communion and communication with his creatures.

In Genesis, for example, God speaks with Adam and Eve and tells them what their role in life is to be: "Be fruitful and increase in number, fill the earth and subdue it. Rule over the fish of the sea and the birds of the air and over every living creature that moves on the ground" (Genesis 1:28). So God "put [Adam] in the Garden of Eden to work it and take care of it" (Genesis 2:15).

The Scriptures that follow these first chapters of Genesis record many encounters between God and the people he created. The role of human beings gets fleshed out greatly as God reveals through his prophets just how his people are to live. The Ten Commandments, for example, are just a taste of the often elaborate instructions God lays out for those who wish to please him (and thereby, by the way, be good).

At the beginning of human history, therefore, the way before our "first parents" lay clear. They were not apprised of all God would want his people to know and be, but they had every reason to make a good start on what might be a long process. To be good was simply to obey God's mandate, to be who God wanted them to be.[13] And so it would continue to be had not the first pair decided to step out on their own.

In short, Christianity does not have a problem of good. That is readily explained. The major ethical problem in Christianity lies elsewhere, as we will see in the following chapter.

Can We Be Good Without a Personal God?

It is all but unthinkable that today one person could be, all at the same time, an intellectual, a dramatist and an admirable politician. But there is at least one. After the Velvet Revolution in Czechoslovakia in 1989, the frequently jailed dissident Vaclav Havel emerged as a man for his time. He became the first president of the new republic of Czechoslovakia and later, when the country was divided, over the newer Czech Republic. Here I want to look not at his political career as a dissident or as a public servant, but rather at his ethical philosophy, one aspect of his life and character that has made him so attractive both inside and outside his own country.

Havel made his debut in the United States with a speech to Congress. He told the combined House and Senate:

> The only genuine backbone of all our actions—if they are to be moral—is responsibility, responsibility to something higher than my family, my country, my company, my success. Responsibility to the order of Being, where all our actions are indelibly recorded and where, and only where, they will be properly judged.[14]

In this speech, in brief, Havel states the ethical foundation for his public philosophy. Responsibility, he argues, must be rooted in a reality that has more than a naturalistic dimension. Here he calls this foundation "the order of Being"; elsewhere he refers to it as the "ultimate horizon." In the published collection of his letters to his wife written while he was in prison, Havel explains some of the background to his view. He ponders why, when he boards a streetcar without a conductor, he always feels guilty when he considers not paying the fare. He comments about the interior dialogue that ensues:

Who, then, is in fact conversing with me? Obviously someone I hold in higher regard that the transport commission, than my best friends . . . and higher, in some regards, than my self. . . . [It is] someone who "knows everything" (and is therefore omniscient), is everywhere (and therefore omnipresent) and remembers everything; someone who, though infinitely understanding, is entirely incorruptible; who is for me, the highest and utterly unequivocal authority in all moral questions and who is thus Law itself; someone eternal, who through himself makes me eternal as well, so that I cannot imagine the arrival of a moment when everything will come to an end, thus terminating my dependence on him as well; someone for whom I would do everything. At the same time, this "someone" addresses me directly and personally (not merely as an anonymous public passenger, as the transport commission does).[15]

We would certainly imagine from this that Havel believes he is being addressed by God. Surely a being who is omniscient, omnipotent, omnipresent and good, and who addresses him directly and personally, must himself ("itself" just does not fit these criteria) be personal. Yet Havel immediately draws back from this conclusion:

But who is it? God? There are many subtle reasons why I'm reluctant to use that word; one factor here is a certain sense of shame (I don't know exactly for what, why and before whom), but the main thing, I suppose, is a fear that with this all too specific designation (or rather assertion) that "God is," I would be projecting an experience that is entirely personal and vague (never mind how profound and urgent it may be) too single-mindedly "outward," onto that problem-fraught screen called "objective reality," and thus I would go too far beyond it.

In an earlier letter he further explains why *God* seems the wrong word for whom or what he has encountered: "God, after all, is one who rejoices, rages, loves, desires to be worshiped: in short, he behaves too much like a person for me."[16]

It is clear from numerous passages in Havel's letters that what he experiences as "the order of Being" or "absolute horizon" is personal.[17] Yet he consistently refuses to conclude that this being is in reality what he experiences. One reason is that he does not "like" who he takes "God" to be. Another type of reason is that he fears that his experience of absolute Being may just be a subjective apprehension of what is not objectively there.

Let us examine the first set of reasons, his reticence to acknowledge a God who "rejoices, rages, loves, desires to be worshiped." For God to *rejoice* means that he takes the good that happens with delighted seriousness. He is pleased. For God to *rage* means that he takes evil with deadly seriousness in terms we can understand as human beings. Rage need not mean uncontrolled anger and vindictiveness. It may well rather be the necessary flip side of God's allowing human beings a large measure of freedom. For God to *love* means for God to intend the very best for us. In fully Christian terms, it means for God in Jesus Christ to give his life for us. For God to *desire to be worshiped* is no more than for God to want us to recognize who he really is—our Creator. We owe our very being to him. He gave us freedom. He rescued us when we failed to live righteous lives. He deserves to be worshiped and rejoices when we do so. It may well be that God desires us to worship him more for our benefit than for his own. Besides, if an artist can justly be praised for a glorious painting, a dramatist for a brilliant and witty play, why not a Creator and Redeemer for his redemption? Havel should surely understand this.

The second major reason Havel gives for not acknowledging a fully personal God is his fear that much of his experience is merely subjective. To be sure, it may be impossible to be absolutely certain how much of our experience is attributable to us as subjects and how much to the object of experience. But some estimates are more plausible than others. Havel is, we note, certain about the existence of an "absolute horizon" that appears to him as personal. Atheists or naturalists would simply say that all of his experience of such a Being is the result of his own subjective self. Why is he so certain? Presumably, he is certain because it is the most plausible explanation of his experience. But why stop halfway? Is it not more plausible that his feelings of being encountered personally by the absolute horizon are caused by the personhood of the "horizon" than that this experience is merely subjective?

What Havel does not seem to see is that the personality of the absolute horizon is a necessary aspect of any foundation for morality. Responsibility is possible *if* there is a person to be responsible to. We are all bound by the "law of gravity," but we are not responsible to it. If responsibility exists, so does a personal God.

This latter is in fact the essence of the problem of finding a foundation for ethics in an impersonal "moral realm" or "transcendent principle" or Absolute. The idea of responsibility demands a person to whom to be responsible. The existence of an absolute Being is, therefore, not a sufficient foundation for ethics. The Christian conception of God supplies that demand. No abstraction can.

There are other aspects of the ethics of Christian theism that point not just to its explanatory power but also to its supremacy. Jesus, for example, is the supreme revelation of God's moral character. It is in his life and teachings that the essential elements of a moral life are most clear. Christianity provides not only a foundation for ethics but also a delineation and exemplification of what a "good" life is like. Moreover, Christianity provides a motivation for living the good life. That motivation is not the fear of damnation (for it is not living a good life that qualifies one for heaven but rather the grace of God, who accepts us even as sinners). The believer's motivation is his or her developing desire to please God and to live for his glory.

The Best Explanation
Ethics is only one of many subjects that can best be understood in a

Christian frame of reference. Human knowledge, for example, is best explained by the Christian notion of being made in the image of God. Since God is the all-knowing knower of everything, as beings made in his image we can be the sometimes-knowing knowers of some things.[18] Human love has a transcendent foundation in the love of God for us. A raft of books and studies may be consulted to show how Christianity illuminates everything it touches.

In the final analysis, Christianity gives the best explanation of all the tough issues of life.[19]

What then is suffering to the Christian? It is Christ's invitation
to us to follow him. Christ goes to the cross, and we are invited to
follow to the same cross. Not because it is the cross,
but because it is his. Suffering is blessed not because it is suffering
but because it is his. Suffering is not the context that explains
the cross; the cross is the context that explains suffering. The cross
gives this new meaning to suffering; it is now not only between
God and me but also between Father and Son.

PETER KREEFT, *MAKING SENSE OUT OF SUFFERING*

————

The
Problem
of Evil

13

I n the area of ethics there are twin issues: the problem of good and the problem of evil. Naturalists who deny the existence of any transcendent, personal God cannot successfully solve the problem of good. They cannot explain why there is a difference between right and wrong. Why do we insist on calling some actions and some people good?

Christians, and others who do believe in a transcendent, personal God, are faced with the problem of evil. The problem is especially poignant for Christians and other theists who believe in a God who is both good and omnipotent. If God is both good and omnipotent, why is there so much evil, expressed in the suffering of so many people throughout the world? If God exists, God is either not completely good or not completely powerful.

This, I believe, is the toughest question thoughtful Christians ever have to answer.[1] There seem, in fact, to be two sides to the same question. On the one hand is the theoretical problem: how can a good God allow such a painful world? On the other hand is the intimately personal problem: why did my father die in such sustained pain? The former, difficult as it is to address, is the easier to handle. We will begin there.

The Nature of Evil and the Free Will Defense

The problem of evil has long been identified as a major issue in defending the rationality of Christianity. One of the first and, I think, most helpful responses was that of Augustine (A.D. 354-430). The argument goes like this.

If God is good, then what he intends for his creation is good. To conform one's will and action to that intention is good; to act contrary to God's will is evil. God is not responsible for evil; people, to whom he gave freedom to conform or not conform to his intentions for them, "create" evil by their intentions and actions. As Augustine wrote, "The only cause of any good that we enjoy is the goodness of God, and the only cause of evil is the falling away from the unchangeable good of a being made good but changeable, first in the case of an angel, and afterwards in the case of man."[2]

Augustine is, of course, referring to the fall of angels and the fall of humankind. The basic notion is that God alone is supreme being. There is no being equal and opposite to him who exists as evil on its own. In other words, Satan is not self-existent like God but is a created being, an angel who rebelled against his Creator. His evil comes not from who he *is* as a being but what he does with who he is. Evil is the perversion of good or the absence of good. It exists, but not as a thing in itself; it exists as the thoughts and intentions, the action and deeds, of one who does what God does not intend. Evil, in other words, is parasitic on good.

The only origin of evil, then, is the rebellion against God of one or more of God's creatures. Cosmic evil on a spiritual plane originated with the rebellion of Satan and his followers. Human evil originated in Adam and Eve's decision to disobey a direct and understood commandment of God: "You are free to eat from any tree in the garden;

but you must not eat from the tree of the knowledge of good and evil, for when you eat of it you will surely die" (Genesis 2:16-17).

Adam and Eve ate the fruit, and the rest (as they say) is history. From the beginning, then, this rebellion brought the most tragic consequences: broken relations between God and human beings, between Adam and Eve, men and women, men and men, women and women, human beings and the natural order, even human beings with themselves. The apostle Paul, ruminating on the results of the Fall, wrote:

> For although they knew God, they neither glorified him as God nor gave thanks to him, but their thinking became futile and their foolish hearts were darkened. Although they claimed to be wise, they became fools and exchanged the glory of the immortal God for images made to look like mortal man and birds and animals and reptiles. (Romans 1:21-23)

Most evil and its painful consequences have their origin in our rebellion against God. Some say that such a notion—the notion of original sin—is unjust, because it places the cause of human distress not on those of us who are living now but on our ancestors. But we forget that to be human is not just to be an individual—a blank tablet on which we write our own destiny—but to be a part of both a long heritage of people who have gone before us and a huge human family in the present moment. Who we are is, whether we like it or not, tied to the past, over which we have no control, and the present, over which we have little effect. Christianity is honest about the sadness of much of human life. The Bible is brutally honest about the despicable evils people perpetrate on each other. Read the book of Judges if you think the Bible is a book of gentle fairy stories.

We also fail to recognize just how profoundly evil evil really is. God is good—all the good that could ever be.[3] To move against the good is not just a mistake that we recognize and apologize for. It is to take who we are—people made like God—and say to God and ourselves that we are not satisfied with our condition. It is profoundly evil to reject the profoundly good. The consequences are justifiably profound.

Essentially, the consequences are built into the rebellion itself. In effect, God says, "Okay. You have rejected me, your own selves; you have rejected the nature of your Creator and of creation itself. Then I leave you in your state of rebellion. If you wish to do things your way, go to it. You have rejected the goodness, the wisdom and the truth that reside fundamentally in me. With that gone, you will not even know what your true end is, let alone be able to realize it." The consequences of rejecting the good are the pain and suffering we see so rife around us and in us.

Some would say that human freedom, the ability to choose not to follow our Creator's intentions for us, can account for most of the pain we experience, but not all. What about "natural evil," the pain and suffering caused by famine, floods, volcanoes, lightning and other natural phenomena? The Bible is, so far as I can tell, silent on this issue. Still, it is at least possible that if human beings had continued in the will of God, they would have discerned the limits set by their environment. The ravaging effect of floods could be prevented if we avoided living on floodplains. Famine is often a consequence of bad farming, not just erratic weather. Had we not fallen, perhaps we would have been better farmers and better predictors of future weather. Volcanoes and earthquakes seem harder to predict, but who knows what we might know about our environment had we developed science and technology as unfallen creatures?

The point is that in creating people with the dignity of free will (thus imaging the full dominion of God over his creation), a good God has not done something for which he is morally culpable. He could have created beings who always chose to do what God intended, but they would have been like robots, creatures programmed never to make mistakes, fail or rebel. But then they would not have borne nearly so much of God's image as do beings who are free to act on their own.

In his goodness he has, rather, created beings who could have chosen to love and serve the good and the true, who could have been "his people," showing in their relationships the glorious goodness of a God of love. But his very goodness has involved him in allowing the consequences of rebellion to take their toll. God's judgment is not the expression of a vindictive God but of a loving God who cannot let rejection of the good and the true finally be a part of his world.

Jesus and Redemption

Jesus in the Gospels, as we saw in earlier chapters, constantly spoke of the "kingdom of God." By this he meant the reign of God over all creation such that all his intentions are finally realized. The Hebrew Scriptures' declaration "I will walk among you and be your God, and you will be my people" (Leviticus 26:12) looks forward to the time when God will finally have accomplished his purpose with creation and with erring humankind. Because of our rebellion, of course, something beyond our creation in his image is needed. With the Fall comes the necessity for a further work of God. That in Scripture is called *redemption,* and it plays a major part in any fully Christian response to the problem of evil.

It is conceivable that a "merely" good God, having given his creation a choice, should simply have left us to go our own way—a way that in the beginning he called "death" (Genesis 2:17). Death is essentially separation. Physical death is the separation of our selves, our souls, from our bodies; spiritual death is the separation of our souls and bodies from God. The consequences of rebellion against God is spiritual separation from God, separation from the only person who can ever satisfy. "Thou hast formed us for Thyself, and our hearts are restless till they find rest in Thee," Augustine wrote.[4] What then is hell but a separation from God marked by foreverness?

But God is not a merely "good" God. He is what we could never have known or imagined without his telling and showing us. He is a gracious God. He called Abraham to found a new nation that would be his people, a special conduit through whom all the world would be blessed. He called Moses to deliver those people from bondage in Egypt. He called prophets to remind the people of God's actions in their own history. And finally he sent his Son, Jesus Christ, to embody most fully who he is, to confirm the teachings he wants us to know, to die for us as an eternal sacrifice for our rebellion. Then he woos us yet today by the Holy Spirit and the written Word of God.

God did not intend to lose us. He loved us so much that he took on himself the pain of separation that we justly deserve for choosing against him. On the cross, he took into himself the agonized experience of the psalmist who called out to God: "My God, my God, why have you forsaken me?" (Psalm 22:1; Mark 15:34). The apostle Paul, reflecting on Jesus' work on the cross, wrote: "God demonstrates his own love for us in this: While we were yet sinners, Christ died for us" (Romans 5:8). Jesus explains why he would die as giving his life as a "ransom for many" (Mark 10:45). Jesus stood in for us—the guiltless for the guilty. In this regard one of the best-known verses in the Bible should be quoted: "God so loved the world that he gave his one and only Son, that whoever believes in him shall not perish but have eternal life" (John 3:16).

It is because God himself in Jesus Christ participated in the sin and suffering of the world that Christians can have confidence that, after all, God is not just good but outlandishly good. Pain and suffering are our doing. Redemption from the causes of our pain and suffering is God's doing. Salvation from our deserved end—eternal separation from God—is a gift. In this sense the kingdom of God has come: the redeemed are already participating in the reality of God's presence.

Yet in historical terms the final salvation of human beings is still on the way. The kingdom of God is coming. Glimpses of this kingdom are given us in the final chapters of Isaiah and in Revelation. We see, undoubtedly in somewhat symbolic form, something of the kingdom's character. These glimpses are enough to give some substance to our longing for peace and joy, goodness and fellowship among people of all races and nations, the end to suffering and the realization of the good intentions of the great, good and gracious God.

In short, one Christian response to the theoretical problem of evil is this: (1) evil is the rejection of the good intentions of God; (2) human beings created free to accept or reject God chose and still choose the latter; (3) suffering and pain are the justified consequences; (4) out of his graciousness God has dealt with these consequences; (5) evil is thus an aberration of goodness that ultimately is eliminated as goodness triumphs.[5]

The Personal Problem of Evil

But a Christian answer to the theoretical problem of evil often is not an effective answer to the personal problem of evil. I framed the problem above out of my own recent experience: why did my father die in such sustained, ever-increasing pain?

The problem comes in so many forms that no single way of answering will suffice. For C. S. Lewis it was the death of his wife. At that point Lewis, having already "solved" the theoretical problem in an earlier book, *The Problem of Pain,* faced the issue in a personal form that did not yield to the same analysis.[6] How he dealt with this is recorded in *A Grief Observed.*[7]

The problem can only be answered in the context of the specific questioner. For it is by its nature a intimate problem. Let me, therefore, tell you how I have dealt with it.

Of course, you need first to know how it hit me. My father, a longtime hypochondriac who was often ill, lay dying in a nursing home three hundred miles from where I live. I had seen him several times over the six or so months after it was discovered that what was making him uncomfortable was a form of bone cancer. This kind of cancer, so I was told, expands the marrow of the bones so that ever-increasing pressure is put on the bone casing, leading to ever-increasing pain. There is no cure. There is not even a pain reliever that can be directed to the cause.[8] Only general pain relievers—various forms of morphine, for example—can even begin to give relief, and along with the relief come a gradual numbing of the other senses and a dumbing-down of the mind. With ever-increasing doses for the ever-increasing intensity comes a loss of awareness of surroundings, of time, of people—a loss of anything other than the pain. One either sleeps or suffers.

Except for the last twenty-six hours, I was with my father during the final week of his life. I had been with him for another week just a month earlier. I saw him go from a normal person with normal interests, though often in pain, to an ever-bonier body, ever less fully human. The few days before his death were torture for him.

"Jim," he would call out, "help me. Help me!" I would stand by the bed, hold his hand, talk to him, pray for him, attempt to comfort him.

"Lord, help me!" he would say over and over. "Won't someone help me? Jim, help me!"

Then occasionally, "Why do I have to suffer so? Why? What did I do to deserve this?"

My understanding of the theoretical problem of evil and of pain did nothing to relieve either his agony or my own. It did give me a perspective in which to place the experience, but I was silent in the face of my father's plea. I could only say, "You did nothing to deserve this, Dad, nothing." Then I would pray, "Please, Lord, take my father. He is yours. He has told me that he loves Jesus. He is yours. Take him."

In due course, my father died. In due course, we all die, some unexpectedly in accidents, some quietly in sleep, some suddenly in massive heart attacks or strokes, some in great pain over a long period of time. I am comforted by the universality of death. That eventually it takes all of us. There is that respite. Pain is not forever. But this is a comfort everyone can take—Christian or atheist.[9] What comfort, what specifically Christian "answer," is there for the personal problem?

I was drawn to Jesus; I am drawn to Jesus. He has gone through such pain as no other human being has ever experienced. He took on himself all the sins of the world, my father's sins, my sins, and he bore for both of us the experience of separation from God. He who called God *Abba*, Daddy, found himself abandoned. "God made him who had no sin to be sin for us, so that in him we might become the righteousness of God" (2 Corinthians 5:21). I cannot fathom such love. I cannot say to a God who has done this that he has treated me or my father wrongly.

It is not fair that my father should die in such pain, I say, and justly so. But it is also not fair that Jesus should have died in such pain. Still, the story of humankind in Scripture is fair to our experience. And it is more than fair that God should do for us what we cannot do for ourselves. On our own we head inevitably away from the One in whom our ultimate joy lies. Realistic to the situation, the Bible presents a God who knows that situation and deals with it in the most gracious way possible.

Jesus is the best reason for believing in the truth of the Christian faith. Jesus is the best reason for seeing how the personal problem of evil can be effectively answered, not finally with a system but with a Person who shows us the nailprints in his hands and the wound in his side.

Taking Evil Seriously

Gloomy Hamlet put the human condition in bold perspective:

> What a piece of work is man! How noble in reason! How infinite in faculty! In form and moving how express and admirable! In action how like an angel! In apprehension how like a god! The beauty of the world! The paragon of animals! And yet, to me, what is this quintessence of dust? Man delights me not—no, nor woman neither.[10]

Christianity explains what Hamlet saw. It explains the ambiguity of human nature: our glory and our wretchedness. We are great inasmuch as we have been created in the image of God; we are wretched inasmuch as we have turned from the Creator to the creation. Christianity takes evil seriously; it acknowledges the broken, wretched character of human beings and explains why they are that way; it acknowledges as well the vestiges of goodness that are expressed in love and compassion and explains why people actually do have these qualities. That is, Christianity addresses and answers both the problem of good and the problem of evil.

In a yoga book a Christian prayer, the "Our Father,"
was suggested as an exercise. The very prayer that Our Lord
himself prayed. I began to say it as a mantra, automatically and
without expression. I said it about six times, and then I was
suddenly turned inside out. I understood—not with my ridiculous
understanding, but with my whole being—that he exists.
He, the living, personal God, who lives in me and all creatures,
who has created the world, who became a human being out of
love, the crucified and risen God.

TATIANA GORICHEVA, *TALKING ABOUT GOD IS DANGEROUS:*
THE DIARY OF A RUSSIAN DISSIDENT

————

The
Personal
Experience
of Christians

14

E very Christian has a story to tell. The details will vary widely, but almost all of them will follow one basic outline: once I was lost; now I am found. For some the lostness is experienced as indulgence in what almost everyone would call sin and degradation. For some it is primarily an experience of loneliness and incompleteness, something missing from life. For some it is the profound sense of meaninglessness, a despair of find any purpose that would make life worth living. For others it is the gradual recognition that though life is not bad, something more is beckoning, something so wonderful that the longing to reach it dominates the soul. A very few, usually those who come to faith as young children, slip from lost to found so easily that in looking back they can hardly remember when they did not feel accepted by God.

For some being found is a sudden experience, a transition from profound feelings of guilt to deep feelings of forgiveness: a woman anoints the feet of Jesus with costly perfume and dries them with her hair. For some it is a sense of coming home, of acceptance into a family with God as Father: a prodigal son returns to a waiting father. For some it is the great relief of finding fresh meaning and purpose: a fisherman leaves his nets and follows Jesus; a tax collector restores all he has gotten by fraud and more.

We turn, then, in this chapter to listen to and consider the impact of some of the stories of how Christians came to believe. Let's begin with Tatiana Goricheva.

Tatiana Goricheva: A Search for Meaning

In the 1970s Tatiana Goricheva was a brilliant philosophy student in the University of Leningrad (now St. Petersburg). She and her colleagues had long given up any hope in the Marxist-Leninist teaching that had been the core of her education throughout her life. Reading the existentialists—Sartre, Camus, Heidegger—and their forebear Nietzsche had been their first "taste of freedom, the first public discussion that was not forbidden."[1] With these philosophers, Goricheva took a firm step forward to faith:

> For all his hostility to religion Sartre could bring us to the verge of despair at which faith begins. His central idea, that human beings make a free choice every second, is indeed a Christian notion. For God wants the free love of human beings, and out of respect for our free decision he has not yet abolished even evil from the world.

Goricheva and her friends with great joy threw off the chains that had bound them to Marxist-Leninist ideology, communist society, the system that had so destroyed hope in them. Though there was nothing yet to replace the clichés of the past, a place was being prepared, at least in Goricheva's heart, for Christ to enter. "The bitter, fearful, sorry truth was more important to me than anything else. Nevertheless my existence was still divided and contradictory. I still delighted in contrast and the absurd, the imponderables of life."

She enjoyed being considered a " 'brilliant' student, the pride of the philosophy department" and would engage in heavy, sophisticated conversations with fellow intellectuals at academic conferences. But her evenings were spent carousing in bars with the low life, "thieves, psychological cases and drug addicts." With her friends she even "broke into a house, just for the fun of drinking a cup of coffee and then vanishing again."

One professor, Boris Mikhailovich Paramonov, worried that she was close to the abyss of despair, challenged her:

Tatiana, why are you trying to destroy everything? Don't you understand that this delight in destruction has always been the bane of Russian thought? Look, we live in a world in which nihilism has already won a complete victory. . . . [Here he referred to the empty shelves in the Soviet market and the red banners with banal slogans.] It's already been achieved by the Bolsheviks. Completely. What do you want to add?

But Paramonov had no positive guidance to offer. Later he emigrated to America.

Though it was temporary relief, her interest in Eastern philosophy did provide a glimmer of hope and a further step forward. "Yoga merely opened up the world of the absolute to me, let my spiritual eye perceive a new vertical dimension of being and destroyed my intellectual arrogance. But Yoga could not free me from myself." While it became "something like a small bridge between the empirical world and the transcendent world," it was a bridge soon crossed. A longing for the best of everything—intellect and spirit—was stimulated in her. She wanted to live on the highest plane, to "become like a god." But all her yogic meditation could not eradicate her base emotions, her hatred and irritation. "The emptiness which had long been my fate and which constantly surrounded me was not overcome. Indeed, it became even greater, became mystical, uncanny, disturbing to the point of madness."

In virtual despair, she contemplated suicide; a number of her friends following the same course took this final solution or became alcoholics or ended in psychiatric wards. For Goricheva, none of these would be the end. The Holy Spirit brought her to life. The story of her crisis must be told in her words:

> I was doing my yoga exercise with the mantras wearily and without pleasure. I should point out that up to this point I had never said a prayer, nor did I know any. But in a yoga book a Christian prayer, the "Our Father," was suggested as an exercise. The very prayer that Our Lord himself prayed. I began to say it as a mantra, automatically and without expression. I said it about six times, and then I was suddenly turned inside out. I understood—not with my ridiculous understanding, but with my whole being—that he exists. He, the living, personal God, who lives in me and all creatures, who has created the world, who became a human being out of love, the crucified and risen God.
>
> At that point I understood and grasped the "mystery" of Christianity, the new, true life. That was real, genuine deliverance. At this moment everything in me changed. The old me died. I gave up not only my earlier values and ideals, but also my old habits.
>
> Finally my heart was also opened. I began to love people. I could understand their suffering and also their lofty destiny, that they are in the image of God. Immediately after my conversion everyone simply seemed to me to be a miraculous inhabitant of heaven, and I could not wait to do good and to serve human beings and God.
>
> What a joy and what a bright light there was in my heart! And not only within me; no, the whole world, every stone, every shrub was bathed in a gentle light. The world became a royal, high-priestly garment of the Lord. How could I have overlooked that before?

This is a dramatic account of a peak experience. Not all Christians experience conversion in such an ecstatic way. But many do.

Tatiana Goricheva did not just "believe" and then live her life as before; she immediately sought instruction in the Russian Orthodox Church, secured a spiritual adviser (a very difficult task in Russia in the 1970s) and quickly became involved in the often secretive spiritual life of Christian political dissidents. Many other students came to faith soon after, some in part because of Goricheva's consistent witness.

They developed a deep sense of community—a community extending back in time and outward in geography and social strata. At her first confession she found herself in "an old stone church, gleaming white and very splendid," standing and worshiping with pilgrim women from as far away as the Ukraine, Kazakhstan and Siberia, and with simple people in rags. "Only here in church did I understand what 'people' means. Only in God can people really be people. And then it also became clear to me that now I am no longer alone, that I too belong to this people, because these unknown people were more akin to me than anyone else in the land."

From this beginning sense of community, she experienced community with the growing number of students who met regularly but quietly to hear lectures on Christianity. Soon after her conversion she, along with several other women, founded the journal *Women and Russia* to help women cope with the desperate situation they face in a godless society: alcoholism, prostitution, poor medical care, cramped life in huge high-rise apartment buildings, long lines for less and less food. Eventually, forced to choose between imprisonment or emigration, she took up exile in Western Europe. There she continued her work for spiritual renewal, struggling to help her new friends—among them secular feminists—to understand that true liberation is to be found only in the context of the Christian faith.[2]

Experience, Content and Reason

Several matters in this account are interesting in light of our concern to see the connection between experience and the truth of Christianity. First, note the honesty, seriousness and intensity of Goricheva's search. She was long aware that life without some meaning other than that provided by Soviet intellectual society or the ethos of Russian low life was not worth living. Yet she had no hint that any worthy meaning was anywhere to be found. Still, she did not do as so many do: abandon the search, numb the senses with alcohol, drugs or, in the West, the ubiquitous Walkman. She kept looking.

Second, note the gradual progression from a glimpse of the truth to the whole glorious reality of experiencing it. Existentialism was a first step forward; it promoted honesty with regard to hope (without God there is no hope). Yoga was a second step; though it fed a false hope for godlike perfection, it rejected materialism and confirmed existence of a spiritual realm. God chose to meet her fully only after she had done all she could to find him.

Third, her conversion was a sudden, not at first "reasonable" grasp that God really existed. How can saying the Lord's Prayer convince one of its truth? God broke through the inadequacy of her own philosophic and theological ruminations and confronted her directly with the reality of his presence. She understood with her whole being that God exists. But what, we might ask, is better than direct encounter? Reason in such a situation comes into play when one asks if what one has experienced merits being considered true. Have I been confronted by reality or illusion? Am I deluded? This must be the first rational response to such an overwhelming experience.

Our own religious experiences and the stories of those of others should be able to pass the test of reflective examination. Otherwise we are likely to be victims of our own desire for meaning. Consider, for example, the experiences Shirley MacLaine recounts in her biographies.[3] One afternoon, MacLaine says, under the tutelage of a spiritual counselor she had a trance experience that lasted for five hours. She saw herself as a young girl, the Princess of the Elephants, in prehistoric India. She takes this to be a veridical account of one of her many past lives. Her only evidence is the experience itself and a subsequent trance experience in which she asked her spirit guide (her own Higher Self, she says) what it all meant. It is a supreme danger to rely on ecstatic experience as its own test of truth. An epistemology of ecstasy must be complemented by an epistemology of reason and material evidence.

As we have seen in earlier chapters, the Christian faith passes all manner of tests for its truth. Goricheva's sudden illumination, her grasp of the truth reflected in the Lord's Prayer, was confirmed in her life not just by subsequent events but also by study and investigation of all that Christianity teaches.

Fourth, notice that Goricheva's conversion was not just emotional. It involved ideas. What was she chanting? "Our Father who art in heaven" acknowledges the existence of a transcendent and personal God (yoga offers transcendence but not a personal god). "Hallowed be thy name" acknowledges that God is God and we are not (yoga assumes the essential identity of us and an impersonal god). "Thy kingdom come" acknowledges that God has intentions for the future of this world (yoga is interested only in the present, not the past or future). "Thy will be done on earth as it is in heaven" calls for God to do his will for us here as well as in the transcendent realm (yoga sees the world as illusory, something to transcend). "Give us this day our daily bread" seeks God's favor in our ordinary lives (yoga directs our attention away from our bodies and their needs). "Forgive us our debts [or trespasses]" acknowledges the guilt of our rebellion against God and acknowledges that he alone can forgive (yoga sees sin as an illusion to be overcome, not a reality for which to be forgiven). "As we forgive our debtors" requires us to forgive others (yoga is private). "And lead us not into temptation" recognizes the continued struggle we will have to be and live as we ought (yoga teaches that those who do good deeds will be rewarded with reincarnation in a higher form and ultimately delivery from reincarnation through absorption into a oneness with God; those who do evil deeds will kept bound in illusion). "But deliver us from evil" admits that the context of our lives is profoundly problematic (for yoga, evil is an illusion). "For thine is the kingdom, the power and the glory forever and ever" again focuses outward on a God who reigns (yoga focuses inward on a god who just is).

At the time of her experience Goricheva was not immediately in a position to analyze the content of her experience. That came later. What struck her was the implicit claim the prayer made to be a response to a personal, transcendent God. And her immediate response was that this was true. When later she considered the evidence for the truth of this claim, she found that it fit into the Christian worldview, which is itself subject to analysis and confirmation.

Finally, we see her immediate involvement with the church. Christianity is not a private affair. We come as individuals, but we enter a family. The fact of the church—the family of God—is itself a reason for belief. Granted, as we saw in chapter three, the warmth of community, the sense of worth that fellowship gives us, the comfort of the personal support of others is not itself a "reason for belief." Lots of communities that are not Christian also offer warmth and support. Christians will insist, however, that Christian community has a dimension that is lacking in other communities. For if Christianity itself is true, then the Christian community is not just a human psychological or social construct but "a sign, instrument, and foretaste of the sovereignty of the one true and living God over all nature, all nations, and all human lives."[4]

Charles W. Colson: One of the President's Men

Charles (Chuck) Colson begins the story of his movement to faith on election night 1972, as he, Richard Nixon and Bob Haldeman celebrated Nixon's landslide victory over George McGovern. Colson, as one of Nixon's closest aides, had worked hard to get Nixon reelected; his efforts had paid off. This evening and the office celebration to follow should have been peak moments, but the three men's subdued mood was instead a harbinger of great depression to come. Colson reflects, "What was spoiling inside me? Just tired? Or was there something very wrong?"[5] It did not take long to realize that the latter was the case; something was very wrong in Colson, the White House, Washington, the whole body politic. Gradually, the tale of the Watergate break-in and the White House coverup came unraveled. Nixon aides began spilling the story, at first quietly to the press, then openly to Senate committees and federal courts.

Though Colson was not directly responsible for the break-in by the Watergate Plumbers (agents appointed to stop information from leaking from the White House), he was intimately involved with those who were responsible, and he had himself engaged in "dirty tricks" to swing the election for Nixon. Even before the Watergate break-in, Colson had been characterized as a "Nixon hatchet man" in countless news stories. "Colson would walk over his own grandmother if he had to," *The Wall Street Journal* said.[6] This quickly became twisted by the media and the popular mind into "Colson *said* that he would step on his own grandmother to get what he wanted." As the investigation into the coverup of the Watergate break-in became urgent and heated, the press became convinced that Colson had been a principal in the coverup, if not the original burglary.

Colson became more and more entangled, first with the defense of Nixon and then with his own defense. In March 1974 he was indicted and later pleaded guilty to influencing, obstructing and impeding the outcome of the Daniel Ellsberg trial.[7] He spent eight months in tough prisons.

His story, written in his book *Born Again*, makes fascinating reading and shows how Colson's conversion profoundly affected his life both before and during his imprisonment. *Born Again* ends at his release, but Colson has continued his Christian service by founding Prison Fellowship to help current prisoners and to improve prison conditions for the future. His several subsequent books have had an significant impact on the lives of tens of thousands of people.[8]

The matter at hand, however, is what led Colson to think that Christianity is true. The key events took place in the summer of 1973, when, as Colson put it, "Watergate's hateful venom was rushing through the veins of Washington."[9] Colson and his wife were getting away to spend a week on the coast of Maine. On the way Colson stopped in the Boston area to talk with an old friend, Tom Phillips. Phillips was a different person, Colson thought, and asked why. Tom then explained how, though he had been very successful in business, having become the president of Raytheon, he had felt a deep emptiness and had read the Bible to find some answers. He said he came to realize that he needed a personal relationship with God, and so, during a Billy Graham crusade in Madison Square Garden, Phillips had turned his life over to Christ. He had been radically changed; he had found a reason to live and had become an active advocate of Christianity.

Phillips then confronted Colson with the arrogance and impropriety of his actions as a Nixon man; Colson fought back but knew his friend was right. He then read a section on pride from C. S. Lewis's *Mere Christianity* that struck home. Phillips had hit a nerve. "*Hubris* became the mark of the Nixon man because *hubris* was the quality Nixon admired most," and there was plenty of hubris in Colson.[10]

> Pride leads to every other vice [Phillips read]: it is the complete anti-God state of mind. . . . It is Pride which has been the chief cause of misery in every nation and every family since the world began. . . . Pride always means enmity—it *is* enmity. And not only enmity between man and man, but enmity to God. . . . As long as you are proud you cannot know God.[11]

Colson's response was immediate: "Suddenly I felt naked and unclean, my bravado defenses gone. I was exposed, unprotected, for Lewis's words were describing me."[12]

As Phillips read, Colson saw his life parade before him. Then Phillips stopped reading and asked if Colson was ready to "accept" Christ as he himself had done at the Graham meeting. Colson demurred but took Phillips's copy of *Mere Christianity* to read later. Phillips then read some Scripture and prayed for Colson. "As Tom prayed, something began to flow into me—a kind of energy. Then came a wave of emotion which nearly brought tears. I fought them back. It sounded as if Tom were speaking directly and personally to God, almost as if He were sitting beside us."

Phillips then waited for Colson to pray. He didn't, but when he reached his car he wished he had; he started to return, but the lights had gone out in the house and he wept as he drove away. Hardly out of the driveway, he pulled to the side of the road, tears blinding his vision.

> With my face cupped in my hands, head leaning forward against the wheel, I forgot about machismo, about pretenses, about fears of being weak. And as I did, I began to experience a wonderful

feeling of being released. Then came the strange sensation that water was not only running down my cheeks, but surging through my whole body as well, cleansing and cooling as it went. They weren't tears of sadness and remorse, nor of joy—but somehow, tears of relief.

And then I prayed my first real prayer. "God, I don't know how to find you, but I'm going to try! I'm not much the way I am now, but somehow I want to give myself to You." I didn't know how to say more, so I repeated over and over the words: *Take me.* . . .

I stayed there in the car, wet-eyed, praying, thinking, for perhaps half an hour, perhaps longer, alone in the quiet of the dark night. Yet for the first time in my life I was not alone.[13]

This was just the beginning of his search. He had yielded to God, but he had very little idea of who the God was to whom he was yielding. In Maine, relaxed and ready to turn his full attention to the spiritual urges that now dominated him, he took a pad and on the top wrote, "Is there a God?" Then he recalled two experiences he had had a long time before. Once in the Navy, aboard ship at night, he stared up at the vast universe of stars, wondering how it had all come to be, and he recalled now that he "had no trouble calling this force God."[14] A second time was in 1966, when he watched his son learn to sail. Suddenly welling up in him was a great moment of joy, and he found himself thanking God for "giving me this son." If he should die tomorrow, he said, his life would be "complete and full."

So much for past religious experiences. Such experiences were what he thought he would be hearing about from Lewis when he read *Mere Christianity*. He was wrong.

What Colson found was a rational argument involving the universality of moral law, the notion of free will and human agency, and the nature and character of Jesus—in short, the sorts of arguments we have been looking at in chapters seven through thirteen. Colson's mind came to be as satisfied as his emotions. By the time the week in Maine was ending, he was ready for a firm commitment of mind as well as heart:

I knew the time had come for me: I could not sidestep the central question Lewis (or God) had placed squarely before me. Was I to accept without reservations Jesus Christ as Lord of my life? . . .

And so early that Friday morning, while I sat alone staring at the sea I love, words I had not been certain I could understand or say fell naturally from my lips: "Lord Jesus, I believe You. I accept You. Please come into my life. I commit it to You."

With these few words that morning, while the briny sea churned, came a sureness of mind that matched the depth of feeling in my heart. There came something more: strength and serenity, a wonderful new assurance about life, a fresh perception of myself and the world around me. In the process, I felt old fears, tension¢ and animosities draining away. I was coming alive to things I'd never seen before; as if God was filling the barren void I'd known for so many months, filling it to its brim with a whole new kind of awareness.[15]

With this commitment Colson had ended his search and begun a new life under a new orientation. He has never looked back. This simple prayer on a seashore in Maine was the turning point.

As with Tatiana Goricheva, the story does not end there. Colson quickly became active in a local church and began to meet regularly for support, fellowship and prayer with a small group of Christians in the federal government. In prison he served his fellow inmates by giving unofficial legal advice and helping to keep peace amid the constant threat of violence. After his release from prison, he founded Prison Fellowship. His subsequent life—the transformation of his goals from pure self-fulfillment to service to others—is itself tangible evidence for the truth of the Christian faith. It embodies the values of the kingdom of God and gives a foretaste even to prisoners of the final glory that awaits God's people.

The Self and the Search for God

What connection between experience and the truth of Christianity do we see in the story of Colson's conversion? First, Colson was not remotely ready to consider the Christian faith in any serious way until his confidence in himself and his self-determined goals had been shattered. His religious experiences had been memorable, but the effects had not lasted. I think that it will always be the case that only those who know themselves as needy—as poor in spirit—will ever be drawn to Christianity. Too much is at stake; one's whole lifestyle is subject to radical change. Pride, hubris, must go. One must be ready to accept that one may no longer be accepted by one's community, even one's longtime friends. It is the desperate who know their desperation.

It is not that Christianity is not true unless one sees it from the bottom up. Christianity claims to be true regardless of whether it is seen to be true. It is just that the truth of Christianity is not seen by those who think themselves in a superior position.

Some people, like Bertrand Russell, do not believe that human beings have sufficient reason to believe.[16] Russell, so legend has it, was once asked how he would explain to God (should God exist after all) why it was he did not believe in him. Russell replied, "I would look him in the eye and say, 'Not enough evidence.' "

I don't know just how God would reply, but I do know that God would be justified in saying, "Berty, you just didn't pay attention. The evidence was there before you all along. You just were too confident in your own powers of discernment, too sure you were right—frankly, just too arrogant to open your mind to what you could have quite easily seen." Some of that evidence is in the life stories of people like Colson and Goricheva.

There is a second element that is just as important as a humble attitude. Colson was not totally unlike Russell. Both were concerned not to believe without reason. Colson did not finally yield his life to God until he was convinced that his belief in God was rational. Thoughtful people do not believe something they think is irrational or silly or stupid. They may well believe more than what they can prove, but they will not believe something they know is not true. Reason is important perhaps more for checking the truth of claims one is confronted with than for propelling a search for an abstract, undefined goal.

Apologetics itself is most useful for those who have already sallied forth on a quest for spiritual reality. It clears away objections to faith as well as providing reasons for it. This is one reason that the best reason to believe in Jesus is Jesus, not some abstract argument about him. One sits and listens or comes and sees. "Nazareth! Can any good thing come from there?" Nathanael asked his friend Philip. Philip responded, "Come and see" (John 1:46). As one hears and sees, one evaluates; the emotions respond to the person, the mind evaluates the data. If one puts oneself in the way of knowing the truth, something of the truth will emerge. That is the testimony not just of Tatiana Goricheva and Charles Colson but of myriad other Christians. We can count on it.

The Testimony of Community

Sometimes the testimonies of Christian communities themselves carry great force in showing that there is good reason to believe Christianity is true. Sometimes the behavior of such communities, sadly, gives testimony in the opposite direction.

A few years ago, I was scheduled to give a lecture on reasons for Christian faith in Ireland. Normally I hand out a sheet listing these reasons, the last of which is the testimony of the church—its embodiment of Christian compassion and love—down through the ages. My host said that in Ireland I shouldn't list that as a reason. I replied that I understood that the Catholic-Protestant controversy certainly appeared to give negative evidence to the truth of the Christian faith, as did the Crusades against the Muslims in the Middle Ages and the present political situation in South Africa. (Actually these are not evidence of the falsity of the Christian faith itself, just evidence that some who call themselves Christians do not act like, and may not be, Christians. Christians have long been charged with hypocrisy; the charge often sticks.) Still, I said, I thought I could show that on the whole the evidence was positive.

I pointed out that there were St. Luke's hospitals or medical clinics in every country where it is possible to have a building with a cross on it. Of course, this did not include Saudi Arabia (an Islamic state) and Bhutan (a Buddhist state). Still, if the possibility opened up, there would be a Christian clinic tomorrow and a hospital the next day. (A bit of exaggeration would help, I thought, to sharpen the point.) But my host would not budge. She clinched the argument with "Well, we have reproduced your list for distribution at your lecture, and we have dropped the last point."

Fortunately, one can point not only to hospitals but to hosts of other illustrations of the argument from community. Take what happened in Sofia, Bulgaria, a few years ago. After the revolution of 1989, a group of about thirty Christian students from California teamed up with an equal number of Bulgarian English majors to learn about each other's cultures. The Christians were typical, lively Americans with a vibrant faith in Christ. The Christians had Bible studies and worship services, inviting the Bulgarians to join them.

No evangelistic pressure was applied to anyone. Still, by the end of the summer, two Bulgarian students had become Christians and wanted to continue the group fellowship after the Americans returned home. When I met these students two months later, there were perhaps ten new Christians in the group, one of whom had not participated in the summer project. They had continued to meet together daily. The description of what they were doing sounded like the activities of the early church as told in the book of Acts.

I asked what had attracted them to the Christian faith. Their response was simply that they saw something in the Christians that was deeply attractive; they had a vitality the Bulgarian students didn't. When they learned that it was new life in Christ and that it was open to them too, they pored over the Scriptures and within a few weeks had met Jesus for themselves.

When a group of Christians lives out their faith in communal worship of God and in care for each other, when they love those around them, especially the outcasts of society, when they serve instead of rule—that is, when Christians show the marks of genuine Christian community—it is indeed a powerful argument for the truth of the Christian faith.

Much of the strongest argument from community will be found in the ghettos and barrios of Two-Thirds World cities and the inner cities of America. Here you will find the untouted work of communities of Christians, individuals and groups engaged in ministry to the poor and the destitute—literacy work, job counseling, child care.

This evidence is not to be confused with sociological cause, as rejected in chapter three above. For this is not the manipulation of belief by others; it is open, direct evidence of changed lives—the changed lives of the Christians engaged in helping and the changed lives of those who are being helped. It is not just in intellectuals that the power of the Gospel is evidenced. Christianity meets both the proper demands of reason and the personal needs of the most deprived. What other religion or ideology can so well substantiate its claim to be true?

Thou has formed us for Thyself, and our hearts are restless
till they find rest in Thee. Lord, teach me to know and understand
which of these should be first, to call on Thee, or to praise Thee;
and likewise to know Thee, or to call upon Thee. But who is there
that calls upon Thee without knowing Thee? For he that knows
Thee not may call upon Thee as other than Thou art. Or perhaps
we call on Thee that we may know Thee.

ST. AUGUSTINE, *CONFESSIONS*

The Challenge of Belief

15

T he task before each of us is awesome. We human beings face the
world without the perfect mental equipment to know and discern
with philosophic certitude just who we are, what our role in life
should be, whether there is a God, if so which God and how we might
find him/her/it. But by the time we know that one of our main tasks
is to answer these questions, the content and equipment of our minds
have already been shaped by our parents, our society and our culture.
We are indeed finite, self-conscious beings, who ask questions that
demand answers necessarily rooted in the infinite.

We are not blank tablets on which reality writes a message that is
clear and distinct. In fact, we discover that there are many answers
to the tough questions we ask and that these answers often contradict
one another. We realize that the thoughts we think with are themselves somehow beliefs, perhaps grounded in nothing but their ha-
bitual use by us and our similarly enculturated friends. Our mental
slate has been inscribed with all sorts of ideas and prejudices. If we

think about the tough questions, we can become quite pessimistic about our state. They can make our head hurt. We can even sink into a despair of ever getting good, true answers to our toughest questions. One student from Amherst seems to have done just that:

To believe is to deceive. If deceit and delusion make you feel good, then what the heck! Everyone knows that belief is merely a creation and fabrication arising from social interaction and the rules it adheres to are mere fantasy. Durkheim and Freud would agree that religion and belief stem from our society. It's our ambivalence toward that which is sacred and unclear which directs our understandings of belief as seen in the totem and taboo relationship.

But such an agnostic approach is actually self-refuting. If to believe is to deceive, then to believe Durkheim and Freud is likewise to be deceived.

The fact is, everyone has to believe all manner of things. It is necessary even to sustain the barest human existence. We live on belief that certain foods are good for us and others are not. Some foods that were once good turn to poison. We eat the good food and avoid the bad by believing beyond final philosophical certitude. We learn, however, which foods have been good for us and which have not, and the beliefs that emerge from this regulate our eating lives.

When it comes to the big issues (does life have any meaning? is there a God to whom I owe anything? why should I live a moral life? how can I know anything at all?), the situation is the same. We are forced to come to some kind of terms with life, to decide how we are going to live and where we are going to seek peace of mind. We are forced to believe whether we want to or not and whether we know it or not.

An End and a Beginning

In this book I have tried to do two things: (1) explain why we should believe anything at all and (2) explain why we should believe the Christian faith. In short, the answers have been (1) truth is the final, governing reason why we should believe anything, and (2) we should believe the Christian faith because it is true. In both cases I have tried to direct attention to good reasons that these are both so. Whether I have succeeded is yours to judge. But I would urge you to do just that, and to do it consciously and with all the passion such judgment demands.

Once we have faced these issues, it is not possible not to judge the answers offered. It is possible, of course, not to judge them consciously or with passion. That is done by countless people all the time. I call them "floaters." They simply go with the flow of their families, their communities, their social group, their culture. If in their social context it's okay to have an abortion, they, giving little thought to it, think so too. If in their social context it's not okay to have an abortion, they, giving little thought to it, think so too. Issue after issue is decided for them. Problems arise only in crisis situations where they are challenged for some reason or other—pricks of conscience, pickets outside the clinic where they are going for an abortion, an ethics class where someone's contrary view begins to make more sense, a TV talk show where the issue is being bandied about. Our society is, however, filled with devices to keep us from thinking critically. The "music" of Muzak, the ubiquitous noise of radio and television, the draw of exercise and sports and games, the intensity of concentration required by our daily jobs: these all conspire to keep us from thinking.

One pundit defined religion as what we do when we are alone. That's not a good definition of religion per se, because it ignores the public dimension of faith. But it does point to the profound individual and personal dimension of belief. When you think about who you are and what makes life worth living, what do you think and why? To contemplate such issues takes quiet and solitude. The first call, then, to those who wish to know why anyone should believe anything at all is to find quiet and solitude.

When the tough questions of life are faced in silence, they can be addressed consciously and with appropriate passion. These questions are not trivial. The process of evaluating the possible answers will evoke emotion. The answers that turn out to be, or seem to be, true will demand response.

Falling into Belief, Deciding to Follow

Coming to believe what one takes to be true is not simply a matter of choice. One hears preachers calling on congregations to believe, to make a choice for Christ. But one cannot simply decide to believe. When the issues are the tough ones, we don't so much decide what to believe as find ourselves *falling into belief*. Coming to believe in the Christian faith, for example, is more like falling in love than like making a conscious decision.

I will give this illustration from the male point of view, the one I am more sure of. First a man notices that a particular woman stands out among all the others. He is attracted to her; he likes the way she looks, the way she talks, the things she says, the way she says them. He begins to get to know her. He asks her out and finds out what her hopes and dreams are. He puts himself in the way of knowing who she is when she is not with others but only with him. He calls her on the phone. They talk for hours. She calls him. They talk for hours. They are both falling in love. They did not decide. They *fell*.

Did they do so without reason? Not at all. The first attraction may not have been very well substantiated by facts, but the final "fall" was preceded by lots of personal experience and the evaluation of shared and unshared values. So it is in the search for the truth about the tough issues. At best they are not resolved with bounding leaps of faith beyond fact, but with consciously putting oneself in the way of coming to know. Belief follows exposure to and evaluation of options. If it is forced by one's own will despite a lack of information and reflection, it is not so much belief as wishful thinking. And sooner or later it will shatter on the anvil of reality. It's the same with a willful unreflective relationship between a man and a woman. "I don't care about all his flaws—I've got to have him!" is a formula for a disastrous marriage and an early divorce—or worse, homicide or suicide.

Still, one does not get married without making a decision. "Will you take this woman . . . ?" "Will you take this man . . . ?" Will you follow your fall with an active participation in the belief into which you have fallen? Some men, some women, just can't, or at least don't, do this.

They stay reluctant spectators of their own beliefs. Eventually, it is fair to say that they really have not fallen in love at all. They are playing with a profound relationship.

With belief comes responsibility. If she is really all I believe her to be, she should be my wife. If he is all I really believe him to be, he should be my husband. If I believe Christianity to be true, I should take it as my active guide to life. If I am a rebel against God, I should confess it before God and cease to be one. If Jesus has died in my place, I should openly, freely, even joyously acknowledge that before God and his people. If Jesus tells us the truth about how to live, I should govern my life accordingly.

Doorways to Commitment

Tatiana Goricheva found in the Lord's Prayer a doorway to the truth about God and an experience that fulfilled her dreams and aspirations beyond her wildest hopes. If you have put yourself in the way of knowing the truth as it is presented in Jesus, if you have considered the implications of genuine, active belief, then you may find as she did that this prayer will open the truth to you:

Our Father in heaven,
hallowed be your name,
your kingdom come,
your will be done
    on earth as it is in heaven.
Give us today our daily bread.
Forgive us our debts,
    as we also have forgiven our debtors.
And lead us not into temptation
but deliver us from the evil one.
For yours is the kingdom and the power
    and the glory forever. Amen. (Matthew 6:9-13)[1]

They do not come with the authority of Jesus, but the simple prayers Charles Colson prayed as he moved to faith in Christ would also be appropriate. The first confirmed his primitive belief that there is a

God and showed his commitment to search for the truth and to take the consequences:

> God, I don't know how to find you, but I'm going to try! I'm not much the way I am now, but somehow I want to give myself to You. . . . *Take me.*[2]

The second prayer, prayed after he had spent many hours reading the Bible and C. S. Lewis's *Mere Christianity,* confirmed his commitment to Jesus Christ as Lord and Savior:

> Lord Jesus, I believe You. I accept You. Please come into my life. I commit it to You.[3]

Goricheva's and Colson's lives were transformed. They have not found living the Christian life easy or even safe. Goricheva was persecuted in Soviet Russia, Colson has spent many more hours in prison with prisoners than most of us would find comfortable. But neither would give up their belief for all the cushy living in the world.

I think the evidence for the truth of Christianity is overwhelming. I have no hesitation in stating that if anyone is willing to do the following and all it implies, they will find this out for themselves. So to those who have not yet believed the Christian faith, let me urge you to do these two things:

1. Read carefully the Gospels of Mark, Luke, Matthew and John.

2. Pray as you do this: "God, if there is a God, please help me discern whether what I am reading is true or not. I am willing to act on whatever I perceive as true."

Everything else that you might do to discern the truth of the Christian faith is secondary. Still, there are other things you may add to the above.

3. Read some of the books recommended in the bibliography at the end of this book, especially those dealing with issues that are not clear to you or about which you have reason to doubt.

4. Talk to some Christians whom you know to be devout in their faith and whose actions do not belie their words. Ask them to tell you the story of how they came to believe and why they believe now.

5. Attend worship services in a church where the Bible is taken as

a sure guide to the truth about God and his world.

As we read in John 1:46, the essence of this apologetic is the words of Philip as he answered his friend Nathanael's question, "Can any good thing come out of Nazareth?" Philip said, "Come and see."

Notes

Preface
[1]Lesslie Newbigin, *The Gospel in a Pluralist Society* (Grand Rapids, Mich.: Eerdmans, 1989), pp. 47-48.
[2]The Gospel of John opens with the notion of God as Logos (the Word), meaning (among a rich array of other implications) "the principle of rationality." See Leon Morris, *The Gospel According to John* (Grand Rapids, Mich.: Eerdmans, 1971), pp. 115-26. I have developed the epistemological implication of the Logos in *Discipleship of the Mind* (Downers Grove, Ill.: InterVarsity Press, 1990), pp. 85-95.

Chapter 1: It Makes My Head Hurt
[1]From *A Source Book in Chinese Philosophy*, trans. Wing-tsit Chan (Princeton, N.J.: Princeton University Press, 1963), p. 190.
[2]And more subtle than we can deal with in depth in this book. If you want to pursue the matter further, I suggest the following general treatises as well as those appearing in endnotes throughout this book: David L. Wolfe, *Epistemology: The Justification of Belief* (Downers Grove, Ill.: InterVarsity Press, 1982); Basil Mitchell, *The Justification of Religious Belief* (New York: Oxford University Press, 1981); and Alvin Plantinga and Nicholas Wolterstorff, eds., *Faith and Rationality: Reason and Belief in God* (Notre Dame, Ind.: University of Notre Dame Press, 1983).
[3]I am thinking here of those scientists who are "scientific realists"—that is, those (and they are still in the majority in universities and research laboratories) who hold that the natural sciences give us knowledge about an external world and not just a language game played by scientists or an elaborate set of more or less coherent intellectual models.
[4]Aristotle *Metaphysics* 1. 1. 980.
[5]As philosopher C. Stephen Evans says, believing in God is not like believing in the

218 _____ Why Should Anyone Believe Anything at All?

Loch Ness monster: "The Loch Ness monster is merely 'one more thing.' . . . God, however, is not merely 'one more thing.' The person who believes in God and the person who does not believe in God do not merely disagree about God. *They disagree about the very nature of the universe"* (*The Quest for Faith* [Downers Grove, Ill.: InterVarsity Press, 1986], p. 28).

[6]Keith Yandell points out in his carefully reasoned *The Epistemology of Religious Experience* (Cambridge, U.K.: Cambridge University Press, 1993) that "for almost any religious belief you like, if it is true, some other religious belief is false" (p. 6).

[7]Douglas Groothuis points out that Elizabeth Clare Prophet has a hybrid view; she says a person is reincarnated until he or she attains to a permanent state of resurrection. On the surface it looks as if this view is a genuine third option. But it implies, I think, an incoherent view of who a person is. Christianity holds that each person is made in the image of God and as such is unique—that is, neither is nor can be more than one personality. Resurrection guarantees the uniqueness of each person. Reincarnation denies such uniqueness.

[8]I have dealt in some depth with the issue of relativism of religious belief in chapters 5 and 6 in *Chris Chrisman Goes to College* (Downers Grove, Ill.: InterVarsity Press, 1993), pp. 45-68.

[9]Though these students are real people, these are not their real names.

Chapter 2: Why People Believe What They Believe

[1]Most of the comments from students quoted in this chapter and throughout the book come from written responses to surveys asking the title question of this book: Why should anyone believe anything at all?

[2]David Wright pointed out to me that this appears to be a quotation from *The Princess Bride.* That raises the question of just where students' beliefs themselves come from. If one were to conduct a study of this, I wonder if movies and rock lyrics would not rate rather high.

[3]I have also dealt with this position in *The Universe Next Door,* 2nd ed. (Downers Grove, Ill: InterVarsity Press, 1988), pp. 93-98.

Chapter 3: The Social Context

[1]I am making no judgment about the final destiny of the people in this condition—children and "those who have never heard" the gospel. For a careful review of the positions taken by Christians in the past and today see John Sanders, *No Other Name: An Investigation into the Destiny of the Evangelized* (Grand Rapids, Mich.: Eerdmans, 1992).

[2]For a technical discussion of the distinction between reasons and causes (and other nonepistemic explanations of belief) see Keith E. Yandell, *The Epistemology of Religious Experience* (Cambridge, U.K.: Cambridge University Press, 1993), pp. 119-33, esp. 119-20.

Chapter 4: The Personal Context

[1]The distinction I am trying to make in ordinary language is that between a *moral* or

legal justification and an *epistemic* justification. We are free to believe that New York is the capital of the United States, but there is no epistemic reason to do so.
[2]Douglas Groothuis suggested this in a note to me.
[3]Americans have not totally rejected organized religion as have Western Europeans, says Alasdair McIntyre. Rather, they have "not bothered to relinquish theism because to retain it involves so small a commitment. When religion is only thus able to retain its hold on society, religious belief tends to become not so much belief in God as belief in belief" ("The Debate About God: Victorian Relevance and Contemporary Irrelevance," in Alasdair McIntyre and Paul Ricoeur, *The Religious Significance of Atheism* [New York: Columbia University Press, 1969], p. 21). It's been over twenty years since McIntyre made this comment, but it seems to me that "belief in belief" characterizes the tenor of belief among many students on campuses today.
[4]Shirley MacLaine, *It's All in the Playing* (New York: Bantam, 1987), p. 174.
[5]I have discussed MacLaine's views in some detail in *Shirley MacLaine and the New Age Movement* (Downers Grove, Ill.: InterVarsity Press, 1988); and *The Universe Next Door*, 2nd ed. (Downers Grove, Ill.: InterVarsity Press, 1988), pp. 156-208.
[6]John Lilly, *The Center of the Cyclone: An Autobiography of Inner Space* (New York: Julian, 1972), p. 51.
[7]See, for example, Richard Rorty, *Contingency, Irony and Solidarity* (Cambridge, U.K.: Cambridge University Press, 1989). I have discussed the views of Richard Rorty in *Chris Chrisman Goes to College* (Downers Grove, Ill. : InterVarsity Press, 1993), pp. 62-66.
[8]Albert Camus, *The Myth of Sisyphus*, trans. Justin O'Brien (New York: Vintage, 1960), pp. 3-4.
[9]I have discussed the existentialists' response to the search for meaning in *The Universe Next Door*, pp. 107-34.
[10]For an extensive analysis of the "meaning of life," see chap. 4 of J. P. Moreland's *Scaling the Secular City* (Grand Rapids, Mich.: Baker Book House, 1987), pp. 105-32.
[11]Nietzsche's friend Franz Overbeck, church historian and atheist, reflected in a memorandum: "To me it seems quite possible . . . that he [Nietzsche] did not bring madness into life with him, but that it was a product of his way of life. . . . I could not entirely resist the thought that Nietzsche's illness was simulated—an impression derived from my long-standing experience of his habit of taking on many masks" (quoted by J. P. Stern, *Nietzsche* [Glasgow: Fontana/Collins, 1978], p. 39). If it was a mask, it was one that he did not remove in the final ten years of his life. See also Frederick Copleston, *A History of Philosophy* (London: Burns and Oates, 1963), 8:394. Janko Lavrin in his "biographical introduction" to Nietzsche writes: "[Nietzsche] finally reached a stage at which he imagined himself as standing so high above ordinary mortals that even company or friendship with them would be a kind of pollution for him. On the self-erected pinnacle, where he now stood, the distance from other human beings was experienced no longer as pain but as a source of pride and ecstasy over his own exceptional role among men. . . . Here he fell a prey to another lurking danger—the danger of titanic self-inflation, of megalomania"

(*Nietzsche* [New York: Scribner's, 1971], pp. 108-9). Again, Lavrin writes, "The shadow of the superman was the pathologic megalomaniac. It was the latter who eventually won the victory—at the price of Nietzsche's complete mental breakdown" (p. 110).
[12]Keith E. Yandell notes how very similar intense, introspective experiences are interpreted in contradictory ways by Jains and Buddhists: "The distinctive difference" between the Buddhist who says "It seems to me that I am but a bundle of states" and the one who says "It seems to me that I am an enduring being" is "doctrinal, not phenomenological" (*The Epistemology of Religious Experience* [Cambridge, U.K.: Cambridge University Press, 1993), pp. 296-97.

Chapter 5: The Religious Dimension
[1]William James, *The Varieties of Religious Experience* (New York: New American Library, 1958), p. 293.
[2]In Keith E. Yandell's technical analysis of religious experience, *The Epistemology of Religious Experience* (Cambridge, U.K.: Cambridge University Press, 1993), pp. 21-32, he identifies and illustrates from religious literature five distinct types of intense religious experience: numinous (monotheistic; a profound awareness of a holy and personal God before whom one recognizes one's guilt); nirvanic (Buddhist; a sense of release from attachment and desire); kevalic (Jainism; an experience of realizing one's own godhood); moksha (nondualist Hindu; attainment of oneness with Brahman, the impersonal One/All); and nature mysticism (a feeling of unity with nature and all of the universe).
[3]James, *Varieties of Religious Experience*, pp. 313-26.
[4]Ibid., pp. 324-25.
[5]See, for example, James's quotation from St. Teresa in ibid., pp. 313-14.
[6]It is likely that James selected texts from Christians such as the "old man" (quoted in ibid., p. 321, footnote) because they do record experiences that point toward pantheism. Still, the immanence of God is part of the traditional doctrine of God, and Christians such as St. Teresa and the "old man" have every right to interpret their experience of God's presence as profoundly intimate without concluding that the universe and God are really one in essence.
[7]Ibid., pp. 292-93.
[8]Pascal's experience falls clearly into the category of numinous as analyzed by Yandell, *Epistemology of Religious Experience*, pp. 21-26. In chap. 12 (pp. 256-75), Yandell cogently argues that these sorts of numinous experiences give evidence that God exists.
[9]In his *Pensées*, trans. A. J. Krailsheimer (Harmondsworth, Middlesex, U.K.: Penguin, 1966), Pascal gives a variety of reasons for the Christian faith: fulfilled prophecy, rational reflection, the nature of the universe and of human beings. He lists three "orders" which, variously understood in various sections of the *Pensées*, have both ontological and epistemological significance. The *body* gives access to the world by its senses; the *mind* gives access to the world by reason; and the *heart* gives access to the world and theological truth by charity. See *Pensées* 110, 423 and 424 (pp. 58 and 154).

[10]Shirley MacLaine, *Out on a Limb* (New York: Bantam, 1983), pp. 327-28.

[11]Ibid., pp. 328-29.

[12]In chap. 13 of *The Epistemology of Religious Experience* (pp. 279-321) Yandell analyzes several experiences from the literature of Buddhism, Hinduism and Jainism in which there are significant parallels to many of the elements in MacLaine's experience. His conclusion is that in principle none of these experiences give evidence for the truth of the religious systems from which they derive.

[13]I have analyzed MacLaine's worldview in more detail in *Shirley MacLaine and the New Age Movement* (Downers Grove, Ill.: InterVarsity Press, 1988) and in *The Universe Next Door*, 2nd ed. (Downers Grove, Ill.: InterVarsity Press, 1988), pp. 191-202.

[14]The evidential value of religious experience has been assessed in more detail by J. P. Moreland, *Scaling the Secular City: A Defense of Christianity* (Grand Rapids, Mich.: Baker Book House, 1987), pp. 231-40; and more technically by William P. Alston, "Christian Experience and Christian Belief," in *Faith and Rationality: Reason and Belief in God*, ed. Alvin Plantinga and Nicholas Wolterstorff (Notre Dame, Ind.: University of Notre Dame Press, 1983), pp. 103-34; and William Alston, "Religious Experience as a Ground of Religious Belief," in *Religious Experience and Religious Belief: Essays in the Epistemology of Religion* (Lanham, Md.: University Press of America, 1986), pp. 31-51.

Chapter 6: The Philosophic Dimension

[1]This professor's comment surprised me. I wonder what his experience has been with undergraduate students in his philosophy class. My guess is that some of them either would not understand the notion of truth as a reason for belief or would reject it. This notion of truth requires the understanding of reality as determinate and the human mind as capable of grasping the nature of reality. A professor of philosophy at the University of Texas—Austin remarked that it was the Christians who were the best students in his classes; they seemed to be the only ones who respected rationality and the human mind's ability to discover truth.

[2]See discussion of the "logic of truth" in Mortimer Adler, *Truth in Religion: The Plurality of Religions and the Unity of Truth* (New York: Macmillan, 1990), pp. 10-39. Adler says, "For all who think reality exists independently of the mind and that reality is what it is regardless of how we think about it, the definition of truth is the agreement of thought with reality. What makes a descriptive proposition true is that it corresponds with the way things really are" (p. 21).

[3]I did note the notion of the "two truths" theory (truths of faith and truths of reason) held by the Averroists in the Middle Ages.

[4]His students later told me that this professor is constantly saying (and assuming in other things he says) that all religions—even when they contradict each other—can be said to be true, at least for the adherent. And Douglas Groothuis has noted that the statement "Truth is relative to culture and the speaker" is itself an absolute statement.

[5]In the late nineteenth century the existence of a rational transcendent was challenged and began to be rejected; today a growing number of people are calling the notion

into question.

[6]Douglas Groothuis calls this notion of truth "an epistemic imperative of the most fundamental kind."

[7]Even religions like Zen Buddhism which reject the final reality not only of God but indeed of anything nameable are implicitly making "truth"-claims. They are at least claiming that God does not exist in the sense Christians believe. See Adler, *Truth in Religion*, pp. 48-50.

[8]Ibid., p. 15.

[9]See chapter one of this book, note 7.

[10]Adler, *Truth in Religion*, p. 21.

[11]Groothuis points out that someone could arrive independently at a belief—such as the nonexistence of a substantive soul—without knowing it was Buddhist belief. But it's highly unlikely that such a belief would be accompanied by a set of other beliefs that would also be identifiably Buddhist.

[12]Richard Dawkins, *The Blind Watchmaker* (New York: Norton, 1986).

[13]James Rachels, *Created from Animals* (Oxford, U.K.: Oxford University Press, 1990), p. 1.

[14]One need not turn to the so-called and much-maligned creation scientists to see that Darwinism and neo-Darwinism are in deep trouble. See, for example, Phillip E. Johnson, *Darwin on Trial*, rev. ed. (Downers Grove, Ill.: InterVarsity Press, 1993), and Michael Denton, *Evolution: A Theory in Crisis* (Bethesda, Md.: Adler and Adler, 1986).

[15]Another way to list the characteristics of a "best explanation" is this: (1) consistency, (2) coherence and (3) completeness. That is, a "best explanation" addresses all the issues that concern us as human beings (completeness) and does so in a way that shows the internal coherence of each working part of reality and each explanation of it and without violating the laws of logic. William Wainright suggests, in a more elaborate schemata, that a "best explanation" may have as many as twelve characteristics: "(1) *the facts that the system explains must actually exist* . . . ; (2) *a good metaphysical system should be compatible with well-established facts and theories* . . . ; (3) *it must be logically consistent* . . . ; (4) *it shouldn't be 'self-stultifying'.* . . . ; (5) *adequate metaphysical systems* [e.g., religions] *should also be coherent* . . . ; (6) *simpler systems are preferable to complex ones* . . . ; (7) *good metaphysical systems should avoid ad hoc hypotheses* . . . ; (8) *metaphysical explanations should be precise* . . . ; (9) *a system's scope is also important* [ideally it should explain 'a wide range of phenomena'] . . . ; (10) *one should consider a system's fruitfulness* . . . ; (11) *good metaphysical systems provide illuminating explanations of the phenomena within their range* . . . ; (12) *philosophical theories should be judged by 'their efficacy in the life-process of mankind'* [Paul Tillich]" (*Philosophy of Religion* [Belmont, Calif.: Wadsworth, 1988], pp. 171-73).

[16]David Anderson, philosophy professor at Illinois State University, gives this illustration of *abductive* arguments (i.e., "best-explanation" arguments) in an unpublished paper entitled "The Justification of World Views": "We are all familiar with these arguments in our everyday lives. I find a puddle of water in the living room next to a window, and I wonder 'what caused it?' Since we build our houses with the express purpose of preventing the occurrence of puddles of water in our living rooms and since we

(typically) live our lives with a certain amount of care so as to avoid causing puddles, we need an EXPLANATION for the occurrence of the puddle. Was the window left ajar during a rain storm? Does the roof leak? Did a flower vase spill? Each of these is a POSSIBLE explanation for the occurrence of the water.

"Of course, there are other POSSIBLE explanations: The Pope may have been on a secret visit to Bloomington, was thirsty, found the door to my house open, came in and had a glass of water which he spilled and failed to clean up. Or again, an alien from another galaxy might have materialized in my living room via a matter-energizer, leaving behind condensation in the living room. There are innumerably many logically (and even physically) possible explanations for the presence of the water. Why do I conclude that it is ONLY REASONABLE to believe that the puddle was caused by a leak in the roof? Because I discover that there IS a leak in the roof and that there is a wet streak down the wall marking the path that the water took from the ceiling to the floor" (p. 2).

[17]A very helpful treatment of the entire program of justifying belief is to be found in Basil Mitchell, *The Justification of Religious Belief* (New York: Oxford University Press, 1981).

Chapter 7: The Gospels as Reliable History

[1]We are talking here about what might be called *epistemic responsibility*—that is, what we are justified in believing given our specific situation. Even the simplest of us is responsible for using our mind to the best of its ability. For some, epistemic responsibility will require them to think at the level of a professional philosopher or theologian; for others less challenged by their surrounding culture, the task will be lighter. But certainly those who have the mental capacity to complete a university education are responsible to examine the foundation for their faith and be ready not only to give an answer when challenged but to be the unintimidated bearer of good news—and, thus, sometimes create an atmosphere in which puzzling questions are a natural part of the dialogue.

[2]Thomas C. Oden summarizes (in *The Word of Life*, Systemic Theology 2 [San Francisco: Harper & Row, 1989], p. 220), the typical view of Jesus held by many modern scholars: "Jesus was an eschatological prophet who proclaimed God's coming kingdom and called his hearers to decide now for or against that kingdom. After he was condemned to death and died, the belief emerged gradually that he had risen. Only after some extended period of time did the remembering community develop the idea that Jesus would return as the Messiah, Son of Man. Eventually this community came to project its eschatological expectation back upon the historical Jesus, inserting in his mouth the eschatological hopes that it had subsequently developed but now deftly had to rearrange so as to make it seem as if Jesus himself had understood himself as Messiah. Only much later did the Hellenistic idea of the God-man, the virgin birth, and incarnation emerge in the minds of the remembering church, who again misremembered Jesus according to its revised eschatological expectation." Oden in the following eight pages shows how and why this "modern" view is seriously at odds with

reason. "How such a vacuous, implausible interpretation could have come to be widely accepted is itself perplexing enough. Even harder to understand is the thought that the earliest rememberers would actually suffer martyrdom for such a flimsy cause. One wonders how those deluded believers of early centuries gained the courage to risk passage into an unknown world to proclaim this message that came from an imagined revolution of a fantasized Mediator. The 'critical' premise itself requires a high degree of gullibility" (p. 221).

³See N. T. Wright's summary of the various views of Jesus in chap. 1 of *Who Was Jesus?* (Grand Rapids, Mich.: Eerdmans, 1992), pp. 1-18. Douglas Groothuis has an analysis of the various New Age "Christs" in *Revealing the New Age Jesus* (Downers Grove, Ill.: InterVarsity Press, 1990).

⁴For an excellent bibliography of modern scholarship on Jesus see Craig Evans, *Jesus*, IBR Bibliographies 5 (Grand Rapids, Mich.: Baker Book House, 1992). The story of the development of biblical interpretation and in particular of the search for the "historical Jesus" is told well in Stephen Neill and N. T. Wright, *The Interpretation of the New Testament 1861-1986*, 2nd ed. (Oxford, U.K.: Oxford University Press, 1988), pp. 13-39, 379-403. Also see Oden, *Word of Life*, pp. 197-228.

⁵Paul Barnett, *Is the New Testament Reliable?* (Downers Grove, Ill.: InterVarsity Press, 1986), p. 44.

⁶Recently John Dominic Crossan, along with fellow New Testament scholars Helmut Koester and François Bovon, has challenged this conclusion. See Crossan's *The Historical Jesus: The Life of a Mediterranean Jewish Peasant* (San Francisco: Harper & Row, 1992), pp. 425-26. Crossan notes the absence of any significant manuscript evidence from prior to A.D. 200 and argues that this opens the possibility of a "tunnel" period in which the Gospels were in flux and development. So in addition to the four Gospels, Crossan gives more authority to his own reconstruction of "Q" (a hypothetical document for which there is no manuscript evidence, but which allegedly consists of the sections in Matthew and Luke that are parallel to each other but are not found in Mark) and on a so-called Cross Gospel which Crossan finds in the Gospel of Thomas, a second-century Gnostic text. Scholars have yet to respond in detail to what Wright has called a "highly speculative and contentious view" (Wright, *Who Was Jesus?* p. 12. But Wright brilliantly analyzed Crossan's methodology in a story-form critique at the annual meeting of the Society of Biblical Literature (1992), published as "Taking the Text with Her Pleasure: A Post-Post-Modernist Response to J. Dominic Crossan, *The Historical Jesus,*" *Theology*, July-August 1993, pp. 303-10. We may also expect a fuller analysis in Wright's forthcoming second volume in the series Christian Origins and the Question of God, published by Fortress Press. One must wait, of course, for time to tell, but it is not hard to imagine that Crossan's methodology will become a historical curiosity, as have most previous speculative reconstructions. (I owe much of the content and wording of these comments to Daniel Reid, reference book editor for InterVarsity Press.)

⁷The most helpful modern analysis of alleged contradictions and other difficulties is Craig Blomberg, *The Historical Reliability of the Gospels* (Downers Grove, Ill.: InterVar-

sity Press, 1987), especially chaps. 4 and 5.

[8]Ibid., p. 123.

[9]Ibid., pp. 195-96.

[10]Ibid., pp. 145-46.

[11]Because verses 9-20 of Mark do not appear in some of the earliest and most reliable manuscripts, most New Testament scholars of all theological persuasions believe that these verses (which list other appearances in the area of Jerusalem) are not original with Mark but have been added.

[12]George Eldon Ladd addresses these questions in *I Believe in the Resurrection* (Grand Rapids, Mich.: Eerdmans, 1975), pp. 79-105, as does John Wenham in *The Easter Enigma: Do the Resurrection Stories Contradict One Another?* (Grand Rapids, Mich.: Zondervan, 1984). See also Blomberg, *Historical Reliability of the Gospels*, pp. 100-102.

[13]Donald Guthrie, *New Testament Introduction*, 4th ed. (Downers Grove, Ill.: InterVarsity Press, 1990), pp. 84-89.

[14]Ibid., pp. 53-56, 125-31.

[15]J. A. T. Robinson, *Redating the New Testament* (London: SCM Press, 1976). Most scholars of all theological persuasions do not accept Robinson's radical redating, but his work does show that a late-first-century date for the Gospels is not necessary.

[16]The problem of bias in interpreting any text—whether ancient or modern—is often vexed. What we want to see in a text we find easy to see; what we don't want to see we often don't see even when it is obvious to others. Modern philosophers and theologians have proposed an approach called "critical realism" which takes our worldview and our personal biases and doubts into account as well as those of the writers whose documents form the authority for our conclusions. Critical realism operates in the argumentative strategy of "best explanation" (it seeks to consider all the data we have at hand and to accept as true only the explanation that accounts best not just for the situation in question but also for the context in which the issue is embedded). See N. T. Wright's excellent elaboration of "critical realism" in *The New Testament and the People of God*, Christian Origins and the Question of God (Minneapolis: Fortress, 1992), pp. 31-46. In Wright's words, critical realism describes "the process of 'knowing' that acknowledges the *reality of the thing known, as something other than the knower* (hence 'realism'), while also fully acknowledging that the only access we have to this reality lies along the spiralling path of *appropriate dialogue or conversation between the knower and the thing known* (hence 'critical')" (p. 35).

Chapter 8: Jesus the Reason

[1]The stories of the widow and the Syrian are told in 1 Kings 17:8-24 and 2 Kings 5:1-19.

[2]There is much discussion among scholars as to what exactly is meant by proclaiming "the year of the Lord's favor." It is in some way a reference to the year of Jubilee, which in the Hebrew Scriptures was to occur every fiftieth year: debts were to be forgiven, and land that had been bought and sold in the previous forty-nine years was to revert to the original owners. It was a way of keeping wealth from forever

accumulating in the hands of few. Jesus is alluding to this notion, but it is not clear what his intent is. John Howard Yoder gives at least the gist of the idea: there was to be "a visible socio-political, economic restructuring of relations among the people of God, achieved by his intervention in the person of Jesus as the one Anointed and endued with the Spirit." See his *The Politics of Jesus* (Grand Rapids, Mich.: Eerdmans, 1972), p. 39, and the attending elaboration on Luke 4:18-19.

Chapter 9: Jesus: The Dilemma of His Identity

[1]As New Testament scholar Geraint Vaughn Jones says, "The parable is not a pleasant tale about a Traveler Who Did His Good Deed: it is a damning indictment of social, racial and religious superiority" (*The Art and Truth of the Parables* [London: SPCK, 1964], p. 258, as quoted by Robert H. Stein, *Introduction to the Parables of Jesus* [Philadelphia: Westminster Press, 1981], p. 77).

[2]For example, in the parable of the prodigal son (Luke 15:11-31), we are not told whether the elder son comes into the feast. If he does, he is accepted by his father; if he doesn't, he is not.

[3]Among major Christian denominations, only the Salvation Army and the Quakers do not regularly celebrate the event. This rite is variously called the Lord's Supper, Communion or the Eucharist (meaning "the Thanksgiving").

[4]An excellent book on this subject is Joachim Jeremias, *The Eucharistic Words of Jesus*, trans. Norman Perrin (Philadelphia: Fortress, 1966).

[5]William L. Lane, *The Gospel of Mark* (Grand Rapids, Mich.: Eerdmans, 1974), p. 509.

[6]The most famous form of this argument is in C. S. Lewis, *Mere Christianity* (New York: Macmillan, 1952), pp. 55-56. It is also developed at length in Peter Kreeft, *Between Heaven and Hell* (Downers Grove, Ill.: InterVarsity Press, 1982.

[7]We will see in chapter ten how a parallel remark recorded by Luke is itself evidence for the historicity of Jesus.

[8]John A. Sanford, *The Inner Meaning of Jesus' Sayings*, rev. ed. (New York: Harper & Row, 1987), p. 23.

[9]Ibid., pp. 23, 25.

Chapter 10: The Scholars' Quest for Jesus

[1]N. T. Wright in *Who Was Jesus?* (Grand Rapids, Mich.: Eerdmans, 1992), pp. 8-18, summarizes the work of scholars using both approaches; in *The Interpretation of the New Testament 1861-1986* (coauthored with Stephen Neill), 2nd ed. (Oxford, U.K.: Oxford University Press, 1988), pp. 389-403, he pays special attention to the scholarship that takes the second of these approaches.

[2]These are summarized by Wright, *Who Was Jesus?* pp. 2-5.

[3]Ibid., p. 5.

[4]Ibid., p. 7.

[5]See chapter seven, note 2, for Oden's summary and critique of modern scholarship's typical view of Jesus.

[6]Norman Perrin, *Rediscovering the Teaching of Jesus* (New York: Harper & Row, 1967),

p. 39.

[7]Ibid., p. 43. The third criterion is the *criterion of multiple attestation:* one can "accept as authentic material that which is attested in all, or most, of the sources which can be discerned behind the synoptic gospels" (ibid.). The fourth criterion is the criterion of linguistic form: "a saying which shows the idiom of Aramaic, particularly Aramaic poetry, is regarded as more likely to be authentic" (ibid., p. 45). Joachim Jeremias uses this latter criterion extensively in his *New Testament Theology: The Proclamation of Jesus,* trans. John Bowden (New York: Scribner's, 1971).

[8]This is the translation Perrin uses. The NIV translation of Luke 11:20 reads, "But if I drive out demons by the finger of God, then the kingdom of God has come to you." It is obvious that nothing significant rides on the specific translation. John Dominic Crossan, one of the most recent scholars to use the methods of the New Quest, also accepts Luke 11:20 as authentic (see *The Historical Jesus: The Life of a Mediterranean Jewish Peasant* [San Francisco: Harper & Row, 1992], pp. xix, 442).

[9]Royce Gordon Gruenler, *New Approaches to Jesus and the Gospels* (Grand Rapids, Mich.: Baker Book House, 1982), p. 40.

[10]Jeremias, *New Testament Theology,* p. 35.

[11]Martin Hengel, *The Son of God,* trans. John Bowden (Philadelphia: Fortress, 1976), p. 63.

[12]There is some evidence that *abba* was used by Honi the Circle Drawer, another Jewish "prophet" of Jesus' day, and by Hanan, Honi's grandson (Crossan, *The Historical Jesus,* pp. 146-47; and Geza Vermes, *Jesus the Jew: A Historian's Reading of the Gospels* [Philadelphia: Fortress, 1973], pp. 69-70, 210-11). There is also a recent argument by James Barr that addresses the issue from a different angle ("*Abba* Isn't Daddy," *Journal of Theological Studies* 39 [1988]: 28-47). For a summary of the scholarship see Larry W. Hurtado, "God," in *Dictionary of Jesus and the Gospels,* ed. Joel B. Green, Scot McKnight and I. Howard Marshall (Downers Grove, Ill.: InterVarsity Press, 1992), p. 275. If Jesus' use of *abba* is really unique, then we have at least one of the very words Jesus used (his *ipsissima verba*). If not, we have evidence that his language was highly unusual, which makes him a highly unusual man of his time who was agreeing with another highly unusual man of his time. And the evidence still stands in favor of his being who the Gospels record him to be. If, however, Barr is correct that *abba* is rather a "solemn responsible adult address to a father," then Jesus' use of *abba* does not in and of itself point to a view of God radically different from that of others of his time.

[13]As Norman Perrin says, "The victory of God is resulting not in the restoration to a state of purity of the land of Israel and its people, but in the restoration to wholeness of a single disordered individual. The experience of the individual, rather than that of a people as a whole, has become the focal point of the eschatological activity of God. . . . This concentration upon the individual and his experience is a striking feature of the teaching of Jesus, historically considered" (Perrin, *Rediscovering the Teaching of Jesus,* p. 67). Gruenler (*New Approaches to Jesus,* p. 27) agrees with this assessment.

[14]Jeremias, *New Testament Theology,* pp. 29-30.

[15]Klyne R. Snodgrass, "Parable," in *Dictionary of Jesus and the Gospels,* ed. Joel B. Green,

228 _____ *Why Should Anyone Believe Anything at All?*

Scot McKnight and I. Howard Marshall (Downers Grove, Ill.: InterVarsity Press, 1992), pp. 593-94.

[16]Jeremias, *New Testament Theology*, p. 121.

[17]The significance of table fellowship and Jesus' violation of the norms of the time is well described in S. Scott Bartchy, "Table Fellowship," in *Dictionary of Jesus and the Gospels*, ed. Joel B. Green, Scot McKnight and I. Howard Marshall (Downers Grove, Ill.: InterVarsity Press, 1992), pp. 796-800.

[18]Jeremias, *New Testament Theology*, pp. 286-88. See also R. T. France, "Servant of Yahweh," in *Dictionary of Jesus and the Gospels*, pp. 744-47.

[19]I. Howard Marshall, *The Origins of New Testament Christology* (Downers Grove, Ill.: InterVarsity Press, 1976), p. 51.

[20]See Wright, *Who Was Jesus?* p. 8-18; and Wright and Neill, *Interpretation of the New Testament*, pp. 389-403.

[21]See N. T. Wright, *The New Testament and the People of God*, Christian Origins and the Question of God (Minneapolis: Fortress, 1992), pp. 224-26; and Michael O. Wise, "Temple," in *Dictionary of Jesus and the Gospels*, pp. 811-17.

[22]Wright, *The New Testament and the People of God*, in Christian Origins and the Question of God.

[23]At the 1993 annual meeting of the American Academy of Religion and the Society of Biblical Literature, Wright was on a panel of scholars reviewing Crossan's own major work, *The Historical Jesus;* I heard him give a brilliant critique of Crossan's methodology that was well received by the scholars in attendance.

[24]Wright, *Who Was Jesus?* p. 98.

[25]Ibid., p. 99. In *Interpretation of the New Testament* (p. 387), Wright comments: "One of the 'constraints' that must operate on any credible picture of Jesus is that we should be able to say of him: 'Someone who did and said things like that would invite the charge of lunacy'; for the Gospels record such a charge, and the early Church is highly unlikely to have invented it."

[26]Wright, *Who Was Jesus?* p. 101.

[27]Ibid., p. 103.

[28]Craig Blomberg, *The Historical Reliability of the Gospels* (Downers Grove, Ill.: InterVarsity Press, 1987), p. 254.

Chapter 11: The Resurrection of Jesus

[1]J. I. Packer in Gary R. Habermas and Antony G. N. Flew, *Did Jesus Rise from the Dead? The Resurrection Debate*, ed. Terry Miethe (San Francisco: Harper & Row, 1987), p. 143.

[2]Blaise Pascal, *Pensées*, trans. A. J. Krailsheimer (Harmondsworth, Middlesex, U.K.: Penguin, 1966), p. 125 (pensée 310). (I owe this reference to Pascal to a suggestion from Douglas Groothuis.)

[3]Michael Grant, *Jesus: An Historian's View of the Gospels* (New York: Scribner's, 1977), p. 176.

[4]Ibid., p. 176.

[5]Alister E. McGrath, *Understanding Jesus* (Grand Rapids, Mich.: Zondervan, 1987), p. 65.

[6]Gary Habermas in *Did Jesus Rise from the Dead?* p. 23; James G. D. Dunn writes, "Paul was converted within two or three years of Jesus' death, perhaps as little as eighteen months after the first reports of Jesus being seen alive after his death. And almost certainly he received this basic outline of the gospel very soon after his conversion, as part of his instruction. In other words, the testimony of I Cor. 15.3-8 goes back to within two or three years of the events described. In terms of ancient reports about events in the distant past, we are much closer to eyewitness testimony than is usually the case" (*The Evidence for Jesus* [London: SCM Press, 1985], p. 70).

[7]Paul Barnett, "The Importance of Paul for the Historical Jesus," *Crux* 29 (March 1991): 30.

[8]It is interesting that even though many scholars believe the Gospel of John to date in the A.D. 90s, they also believe that some of the accounts of the events during the last week of Jesus' life bear the marks of historicity.

[9]Raymond Brown, *The Gospel According to John,* Anchor Bible 29 (Garden City, N.Y.: Doubleday, 1970), p. 1007.

[10]Because a lot rests on its implications, the phrase *son of man* has been the subject of intense controversy in modern biblical studies. If Jesus used the phrase to identify himself with the "son of man" in Daniel (Daniel 7:13-14), he was making in his day a fairly direct claim to divinity. But many modern scholars have already decided that Jesus could not have actually been such a divine or quasi-divine being. If Jesus made such a claim, this would make him either a liar or one greatly deluded about who he was. Neither horn of this dilemma is convenient for those scholars who want to hold Jesus in high regard as a great moral teacher. The issue is complex enough, however, so that a mere charge of antisupernatural bias against these modern scholars is not sufficient to disprove their claim. See the summary of the argument in I. H. Marshall, "Son of Man," in *Dictionary of Jesus and the Gospels,* ed. Joel B. Green, Scot McKnight and I. Howard Marshall (Downers Grove, Ill.: InterVarsity Press, 1992), pp. 775-81.

[11]McGrath, *Understanding Jesus,* pp. 70-71.

[12]Ibid., p. 73.

[13]Val Grieve, *Your Verdict on the Empty Tomb* (Leicester, U.K.: Inter-Varsity Press, 1988), p. 57.

[14]In John 5:39, Jesus says to the religious leaders, "You diligently study the Scriptures because you think that by them you possess eternal life. These are the Scriptures that testify about me, yet you refuse to come to me to have life."

Chapter 12: The Rationality of Christian Faith

[1]See, for example, C. S. Lewis, *Mere Christianity* (New York: Macmillan, 1952), pp. 17-39; and J. P. Moreland, *Scaling the Secular City* (Grand Rapids, Mich.: Baker Book House, 1987), pp. 105-32.

[2]James Q. Wilson, "What Is Moral, and How Do We Know It?" *Commentary,* June 1993, p. 37: Wilson's essay is a substantial summary of his argument in *The Moral Sense* (New York: Free Press, 1993).

³This question is the title of an article by political scientist Glenn Tinder, "Can We Be Good Without God?" *The Atlantic*, December 1989, pp. 69-85; a fuller treatment can be found in his *The Political Meaning of Christianity* (Baton Rouge: Louisiana State University Press, 1989).

⁴One list of elements that go to make up a good life, a life characterized by happiness in the best sense, is given by Kai Nielsen in his widely read book *Ethics Without God* (Buffalo, N.Y.: Prometheus Books, 1973), pp. 51-54. Nielsen's list includes freedom from pain and want; a sense of security and emotional peace; human love and companionship; meaningful work; the aesthetic experience of art, music and dance; alleviating the suffering of others. Christians should little quarrel with what is listed, though they would wish to add elements not listed, such as a sense of relationship to God and an expression of values that go beyond the merely ethical, such as sacrificial living and loving one's enemies as well as one's neighbors. These latter are commended by Jesus in the Sermon on the Mount (Matthew 5—7) and are aspects not just of happiness in the best sense but of full-fledged blessedness.

⁵Wilson, "What Is Moral?" pp. 38-39.

⁶Ibid., p. 41.

⁷Ibid., p. 42.

⁸Phillip E. Johnson (in "Nihilism and the End of Law," *First Things*, March 1993, pp. 19-25) examines modern legal theory and argues that it has met the "modernist impasse." Quoting an unpublished lecture by law professor Arthur Leff, Johnson points out that people want a "complete, transcendent, and immanent set of propositions about right and wrong" and at the same time want "to be wholly free, not only to choose what we ought to do, but to decide for ourselves what we ought to be" (p. 20). That is, people wish both to be ruled by common law and to make the rules themselves. Johnson's critique of recent attempts to make, under this condition, a coherent theory of law and of ethics parallels the argument of this present chapter.

⁹The attempt to derive value from fact was evaluated some decades ago by G. E. Moore, who contributed the term *naturalistic fallacy* to the effort to do so. See the discussion of this issue in Frederick Copleston, *Bentham to Russell*, vol. 8 of *A History of Philosophy* (London: Burns and Oates, 1966), pp. 408-14.

¹⁰James Rachels in *Created from Animals* (Oxford, U.K.: Oxford University Press, 1990) strives nobly to construct an ethical theory on the basis of naturalistic evolution: "After Darwin we can no longer think of ourselves as occupying a special place in creation—instead, we must realize that we are products of the same evolutionary forces, working blindly and without purpose, that shaped the rest of the animal kingdom" (p. 1). But like the theories he criticizes, his own theory commits the naturalistic fallacy. We intuit certain moral principles, he says. If there were some foundation for these intuitions (for example, that there is a God who is good and has made us capable of intuiting aspects of goodness), then intuition might well explain our common moral motions. With naturalistic evolution, we only have the fact of the intuitions, not the reality of that which is intuited; that tells us nothing about the status of the intuitions, whether they indicate what really is right or wrong. In fact, natu-

ralism in principle cannot do so. Likewise, Kai Nielsen runs afoul of the naturalistic fallacy—after explaining what it is and attempting to avoid it. He writes, "I cannot prove that happiness is good, but Christian and non-Christian alike take it in practice to be a very fundamental good. I can only appeal to your sense of psychological realism to persuade you to admit intellectually what in practice you acknowledge, namely, that happiness is good and pointless suffering is bad" (p. 56). To what does this appeal but to the facticity of one's moral predilections? From the fact that we intuit the good comes the foundation for morality. But our intuitions are only as good as the actuality of what they intuit. If our intuitions are correct, then there really is a nonnatural realm of *ought* from which variation is wrong. But that would mean that naturalism is false, a position diametrically opposed to the one Nielsen holds. J. P. Moreland examines and refutes a further move that might be made by a naturalist— the attempt to ground morality in the notion of "immanent purpose" (that purpose is built into the natural substance of the natural universe). See Moreland, *Scaling the Secular City*, pp. 122-28.

[11]The notion of a pantheistic world, a concept that is itself imbued with the nature of a universal God such as the Hindu Brahman or a pantheon of gods, faces a different problem: how to maintain the difference between good and evil when both are manifestations of the same spiritual reality. Though pantheists, like everyone else, distinguish between right and wrong, they finally have to see these distinctions as local, relative to the changing times, the ephemeral nature of what ultimately must be considered an illusion; God as the One or Brahman is beyond the distinctions between good and evil and thus provides no final foundation for that distinction. I have also commented on pantheistic ethics in *The Universe Next Door*, 2nd ed. (Downers Grove, Ill.: InterVarsity Press, 1988), pp. 148-50.

[12]I am trying here to keep from being impaled on the horns of the dilemma Plato poses in *Euthyphro*, in which one is asked to have either a god whose arbitrary will is the good or a god who is beholden to a standard outside himself. If I had to choose which horn to be impaled on, it would be the latter: God is good because he obeys the norm of absolute goodness. After all, what limitation would it be for God to have such a character that he always chooses the good? But I do not think Plato's dilemma is real: if God is self-existentially what it is to be good, then his intentions as well as his actions, however varied the possibilities of his infinite creativity may be, will always be good.

[13]In rejecting the notion that human beings have or ought to have a purpose that is not of their own choosing, Nielsen says, "To say that a man has a purpose in [the sense of a function or role he is designed to perform] is actually offensive for it involves treating man as a kind of tool or artifact. It is degrading for a man to be regarded as merely serving a purpose. If I turned to you and asked, 'What are you for?' it would be insulting to you. It would be as if I had reduced you to 'the level of a gadget, a domestic animal or perhaps a slave.' I would be treating you merely as a means and not as an end. Failing to have a purpose in that sense does not at all detract from the meaningfulness of life Many of us, at any rate, would be very

disturbed and think our lives meaningless if we *did* have a purpose in this first sense" (p. 40). To me this seems to be a fairly good modern expression of what Adam and Eve did in the Garden—reject the notion of any obligation to fulfill the intentions of their Creator.

[14]Vaclav Havel, "Help the Soviet Union on Its Road to Democracy: Consciousness Precedes Being," *Vital Speeches,* March 5, 1990, p. 330.

[15]Vaclav Havel, *Letters to Olga: June 1979—September 1982,* trans. Paul Wilson (New York: Henry Holt, 1989), pp. 345-46.

[16]Ibid., p. 233.

[17]See my "An Open Letter to Vaclav Havel," *Crux,* June 1991, pp. 9-14, for a more detailed examination of Havel's experience and his refusal to acknowledge the existence of a fully personal God.

[18]For a more extensive development of this idea see my *The Universe Next Door,* pp. 33-36; and *Discipleship of the Mind* (Downers Grove, Ill.: InterVarsity Press, 1990), pp. 79-113.

[19]For a discipline-by-discipline guide to books that show how Christianity illuminates a panorama of academic disciplines and professions, see the bibliography in *Discipleship of the Mind,* pp. 219-43.

Chapter 13: The Problem of Evil

[1]There is a rich lode of books dealing with the problem of evil from a Christian perspective. See the bibliography at the end of the present book for a guide.

[2]Augustine *The Enchiridion* 23, in *The Basic Writings of Saint Augustine,* ed. Whitney J. Oates (New York: Random House, 1948), 1:672.

[3]Augustine calls this "the highest and best good" *(summum bonum)* in *Confessions* 7. 4; in *Basic Writings of Saint Augustine,* 1:94.

[4]Augustine *Confessions* 1. 1; in *Basic Writings of Saint Augustine,* 1:3.

[5]See Marilyn McCord Adams, "Redemptive Suffering: A Christian Solution to the Problem of Evil," in *Rationality, Religious Belief and Moral Commitment,* ed. Robert Audi and William J. Wainwright (Ithaca, N.Y.: Cornell University Press, 1986), pp. 248-67, for a brilliant and detailed presentation for the relevance of the "cross" to solving the problem of evil.

[6]C. S. Lewis, *The Problem of Pain* (New York: Macmillan, 1940).

[7]C. S. Lewis, *A Grief Observed* (London: Faber and Faber, 1961).

[8]The very evening of the day I wrote this sentence, I heard on television news that a drug was just being released; the claim is that one shot (costing twenty-five hundred dollars) will give pain relief for bone cancer that lasts for six months. I count the development of such drugs an application of the values of the kingdom of God.

[9]Atheists can take the inevitability of death as a comfort because—based on the naturalistic premise—there is no life after death. All consciousness of pleasure or pain disappears. If there is a "life" after death, however, the atheist who takes comfort in this life may not take so much comfort in the next.

[10]William Shakespeare, *Hamlet,* act 2, scene 2, lines 315-22.

Chapter 14: The Personal Experience of Christians

[1]Tatiana Goricheva tells the story of her conversion in *Talking About God Is Dangerous*, trans. from the German by John Bowden (New York: Crossroad, 1986), pp. 10-18. Most of the details that follow are drawn from pp. 13-20.

[2]Ibid., pp. 86-103.

[3]Shirley MacLaine, *Dancing in the Light* (New York: Bantam, 1986), pp. 353-59.

[4]Lesslie Newbigin, *Foolishness to the Greeks* (Grand Rapids, Mich.: Eerdmans, 1986), p. 124.

[5]Charles Colson, *Born Again* (Old Tappan, N.J.: Spire Books, 1977), p. 20.

[6]Ibid., pp. 57, 70-71, 189-90.

[7]Ellsberg had been charged with leaking confidential information to the press.

[8]See, for example, *Loving God* (Grand Rapids, Mich.: Zondervan, 1987) and *The Body: Being Light in Darkness* (Dallas: Word Books, 1992).

[9]Colson, *Born Again*, p. 105.

[10]Ibid., p. 72.

[11]Ibid., p. 113.

[12]Ibid.

[13]Ibid., pp. 116-17.

[14]Ibid., p. 121.

[15]Ibid., p. 130.

[16]In philosophy this notion is known as the "hidden God" objection. A technical rejoinder to this objection is found in Thomas V. Morris, "The Hidden God," *Philosophical Topics* 16 (Fall 1988): 5-21.

Chapter 15: The Challenge of Belief

[1]Because the last two lines are so commonly a part of the Lord's Prayer as used by the church down through the ages, I have included them; some (though not the best) manuscripts do include them. See marginal note in the New International Version (Matthew 6:13).

[2]Charles Colson, *Born Again* (Old Tappan, N.J.: Spire Books, 1977), p. 117.

[3]Ibid., p. 130.

Bibliography

These books are subdivided into categories related to but not exactly equivalent to the topics covered in each chapter. Most were still in print when the present book was published; those not in print are worth securing through libraries and interlibrary loans. Those preceded by an asterisk are the more basic.

Why Should Anyone Believe Anything?

Hasker, William. *Metaphysics: Constructing a World View*. Downers Grove, Ill.: InterVarsity Press, 1983. A basic introduction to key issues in philosophy: freedom and necessity, minds and bodies, God and the nature of the world.

Mitchell, Basil. *The Justification of Religious Belief*. New York: Oxford University Press, 1981. A modestly technical treatment of the subject of the present book.

*Wolfe, David L. *Epistemology: The Justification of Belief*. Downers Grove, Ill.: InterVarsity Press, 1982. A basic introduction to how human beings can know anything at all. (Out of print)

The Character of Jesus Christ

*The Gospels of Matthew, Mark, Luke and John in the Bible. See especially modern translations such as the Revised Standard Version, the New Revised Standard or the New International Version. The Gospels are the primary documents and carry more authority than any of the following books, all of which rely on these documents as sources.

Anderson, Norman. *Jesus Christ: The Witness of History*. Rev. ed. Downers Grove, Ill.: InterVarsity Press, 1985. An analysis of the historical evidence for the character of Jesus as presented in the Gospels; includes a section on the historicity of the resurrection.

*Kreeft, Peter, *Between Heaven and Hell*. Downers Grove, Ill.: InterVarsity Press, 1982

An imaginative fictitious discussion between C. S. Lewis, John F. Kennedy and Aldous Huxley (all of whom died on the same day) set "between heaven and hell"; the main topic is Lewis's liar-lunatic-lord argument for the deity of Christ.

* _____. *Socrates Meets Jesus.* Downers Grove, Ill.: InterVarsity Press, 1987. An imagined discussion between Socrates (who wakes up in the twentieth century and finds himself enrolled in a divinity school) and students and professors. Socrates becomes convinced that most of his new colleagues have misunderstood and failed to believe the truth about God, Jesus and the Christian life. A delightful treatment of the central issues of Christian faith. (Out of print)

McGrath, Alister. *Understanding Jesus.* Grand Rapids, Mich.: Zondervan, 1987. A basic, highly readable study of Jesus' character and work.

Sire, James W. *Meeting Jesus.* Wheaton, Ill.: Shaw, 1988. A group or individual Bible-study guide focusing on some of the passages analyzed in the present book.

*Stott, John. *Basic Christianity.* 2nd ed. Downers Grove, Ill.: InterVarsity Press, 1971. The best single book introducing the character of Christianity primarily through its central commanding figure, Jesus.

Witherington, Ben, III. *The Christology of Jesus.* Minneapolis: Fortress, 1990. A scholarly, technical study of who Jesus understood himself to be.

Wright, N. T. *Jesus and the Victory of God.* Minneapolis: Fortress, 1994. A profound scholarly analysis of Jesus using the methodology of the Third Quest of the historical Jesus.

_____. *Who Is Jesus?* Grand Rapids, Mich.: Eerdmans, 1992. A critique of three modern studies of Jesus and a presentation in brief compass of the view of Jesus developed in depth in *Jesus and the Victory of God.*

The Resurrection of Jesus

Habermas, Gary R., and Anthony G. N. Flew. *Did Jesus Rise from the Dead?* Ed. Terry L. Miethe. San Francisco: Harper & Row, 1987. Records a debate between Habermas (Christian) and Flew (atheist) with presentations, rejoinders and comments by other scholars. One of the clearest and most persuasive among modern presentations of the case for the resurrection.

Ladd, George Eldon. *I Believe in the Resurrection.* Grand Rapids, Mich.: Eerdmans, 1975. A scholarly analysis of the key issues surrounding the resurrection. Excellent on reconciling the various accounts in the four Gospels.

Morison, Frank. *Who Moved the Stone?* Downers Grove, Ill.: InterVarsity Press, 1958. A classic treatment by a man who set out to disprove the resurrection but changed his mind.

The Historical Reliability of the Gospels

*Barnett, Paul. *Is the New Testament Reliable?* Downers Grove, Ill.: InterVarsity Press, 1986. An excellent, basic defense of the New Testament as giving a reliable account of the life and teachings of Jesus and of the early church.

*Blomberg, Craig. *The Historical Reliability of the Gospels.* Downers Grove, Ill.: InterVarsity Press, 1987. More detailed than Barnett's book in treating form criticism, redaction criticism, alleged contradictions and modern hermeneutic theory.

Dunn, James D. G. *The Evidence for Jesus.* Philadelphia: Westminster Press, 1986. An excellent introduction to the study of the differences between the Synoptic accounts of the same events and teachings; the question whether Jesus claimed to be God; the resurrection; and the early church from which the Gospels emerged.

France, R. T. *The Evidence for Jesus.* Downers Grove, Ill.: InterVarsity Press, 1986. Surveys the biblical and extrabiblical documents attesting to Jesus.

Marshall, I. Howard. *I Believe in the Historical Jesus.* Grand Rapids, Mich.: Eerdmans, 1977. A New Testament scholar's assessment of what can be known about Jesus.

Wenham, John. *Christ and the Bible.* 2nd ed. Grand Rapids, Mich.: Baker Book House, 1984. A classic defense of the reliability of both the Old and New Testaments, arguing that "belief in the Bible comes from faith in Christ, and not vice versa; and that it is possible to proceed from faith in Christ to a doctrine of Scripture without sorting out problems of criticism" (p. 9).

The Rationality of Christian Faith

*Chesterton, G. K. *Orthodoxy.* Garden City, N.Y.: Image/Doubleday, 1959. Written in the early twentieth century, this witty apologetic work has provided a wealth of suggestive arguments for the truth of the Christian faith.

*Evans, C. Stephen. *Quest for Faith.* Downers Grove: InterVarsity Press, 1986. A philosopher's argument for the Christian faith, accessible to those without a knowledge of philosophy.

———. *Philosophy of Religion.* Downers Grove, Ill.: InterVarsity Press, 1985. A basic (but more detailed than *Quest for Faith*) treatment of the rationality of Christian belief; covers natural theology, arguments for God's existence, religious experience, miracle, religious language, science and faith, the problem of evil and religious pluralism.

Kreeft, Peter. *The Best Things in Life.* Downers Grove, Ill.: InterVarsity Press, 1984. A clever, imaginative dialogue set on the campus of Desperate State University; the topics include power, pleasure, truth and the good life.

Kreeft, Peter, and Ronald Tacelli. *Handbook of Christian Apologetics.* Downers Grove, Ill.: InterVarsity Press, 1994. A "catalog" of arguments for the truth of Christianity.

*Lewis, C. S. *Mere Christianity.* New York. Macmillan, 1958. Brilliantly argued and written, this book is probably the most famous of all modern defenses of the Christian faith.

———. *Miracles.* New York: Macmillan, 1963. A critique of naturalism as an explanation of reality and a defense of the notion and fact of miracles.

Mavrodes, George. *Belief in God.* New York: Random House, 1970. A philosopher's technical treatment of the title topic.

Moreland, J. P. *Scaling the Secular City.* Grand Rapids, Mich.: Baker Book House, 1987. A semitechnical, carefully reasoned defense of Christianity that deals with a wide panorama of issues: the existence of God, the meaning of life, the historicity of the

238 _____ Why Should Anyone Believe Anything at All?

New Testament, the resurrection of Jesus, and science and faith. One of the best
general apologetic works.
Morris, Thomas V. *Making Sense of It All: Pascal and the Meaning of Life.* Grand Rapids,
Mich.: Eerdmans, 1992. A modern philosopher shows the relevance of a seventeenth-century philosopher's apologetic for the Christian faith. Well written and
argued.
Percy, Walker. *Lost in the Cosmos.* New York: Washington Square, 1984. A novelist's
imaginative and clever apologetic for a Christian conception of reality.
Plantinga, Alvin, and Nicholas Wolterstorff, eds. *Faith and Rationality: Reason and Belief
in God.* Notre Dame, Ind.: University of Notre Dame Press, 1983. This collection of
essays on the title topic by philosophers William P. Alston, George Mavrodes, the
editors and others has set the agenda for much subsequent dialogue among Christian academics.
Swinburne, Richard. *The Coherence of Theism.* New York: Oxford University Press, 1977.
A very technical analysis of the case for theism.
_____ . *The Concept of Miracle.* New York: Macmillan, 1970. A technical treatment.
_____ . *The Existence of God.* New York: Oxford University Press, 1979. A philosopher's
technical case for the existence of God. Not for the beginning reader of philosophy.

Alternatives to Christian Faith
Anderson, Norman. *Christianity and World Religions.* 2nd ed. Downers Grove, Ill.: Inter-
Varsity Press, 1984. Presents the uniqueness of Christianity among the world religions.
Moore, Peter. *Disarming the Secular Gods.* Downers Grove, Ill.: InterVarsity Press, 1989.
A basic and readable analysis of contemporary alternatives to Christian faith: hu-
manism, relativism, narcissism, agnosticism, pragmatism, hedonism and New Age
spirituality.
Neill, Stephen. *Christian Faith and Other Faiths.* Downers Grove, Ill.: InterVarsity Press,
1984. An irenic description and comparison of Judaism, Islam, Hinduism, Buddhism
and primal religions in light of Christianity. Excellent for gaining a sensitive understanding of religious alternatives as one sees at the same time the superiority of
Christian faith.
Netland, A. Harold. *Dissonant Voices.* Grand Rapids, Mich.: Eerdmans, 1991. A profound
but easily accessible critique of religious pluralism and relativism.
Sire, James W. *The Universe Next Door.* 2nd ed. Downers Grove, Ill.: InterVarsity Press,
1988. Describes and compares the worldviews of Christian theism, deism, naturalism,
existentialism, Eastern pantheistic monism and New Age spirituality, arguing that
Christian theism gives the "best explanation" for the tough questions of life.

The Problem of Evil
Craigie, Peter C. *The Problem of War in the Old Testament.* Grand Rapids, Mich.: Eerdmans, 1978. Deals very well with one of the major modern objections to Christian
faith.

Kreeft, Peter. *Making Sense out of Suffering.* Ann Arbor, Mich.: Servant, 1986. A master-fully crafted, superbly written exploration of the issues surrounding the mystery of suffering.

Lewis, C. S. *A Grief Observed.* London: Faber and Faber, 1961. Lewis's poignant reflections on the personal problem of suffering as he attempts to deal with the death of his wife from a painful illness.

————. *The Problem of Pain.* New York: Macmillan, 1940. Lewis's philosophic reflections on the problem of suffering.

Wenham, John. *The Enigma of Evil: Can We Believe in the Goodness of God?* Grand Rapids, Mich.: Zondervan, 1985. An excellent study of the issue of evil in both biblical and modern times.

The Personal Experience of Christians

Clark, Kelly James, ed. *Philosophers Who Believe.* Downers Grove, Ill.: InterVarsity Press, 1993. Eleven philosophers (Mortimer Adler, Stephen Davis, Basil Mitchell, Terence Penelhum, Alvin Plantinga, Nicholas Rescher, John Rist, Frederick Suppe, Richard Swinburne, Nicholas Wolterstorff and Linda Zagzebski) recount the spiritual journeys that brought them to belief in Christ.

*Colson, Charles. *Born Again.* Old Tappan, N.J.: Chosen Books, 1976. A Nixon "hatchet man" tells the story of his coming to faith in the aftermath of the Watergate break-in.

*Goricheva, Tatiana. *Talking About God Is Dangerous.* Trans. from the German by John Bowden. New York: Crossroad, 1987. A Russian dissident recounts her conversion from Marxist-Leninism through existentialism and yoga to Orthodox Christian faith.

Ten Boom, Corrie. *The Hiding Place.* Washington Depot, Conn.: Chosen Books, 1971. A Dutch Christian tells the story of the persecution of Jews and her family's role in hiding Jews from the Nazis during World War II.

Vanauken, Sheldon. *A Severe Mercy.* New York: Bantam. The intensely and well-written story of two young intellectuals and their search for truth under the influence of C. S. Lewis.